D0877728

STUDIES IN AMERICAN LITERATURE

Volume XXX

SETTING IN THE AMERICAN SHORT STORY OF LOCAL COLOR

1865-1900

by

ROBERT D. RHODE

Texas A & I University

1975

MOUTON

THE HAGUE · PARIS

PS
374
.S5
R 5
1975

813.09
R47ᵈ

cac

Pq

© Copyright 1975 in The Netherlands
Mouton & Co. N.V., Publishers, The Hague

*No part of this book may be translated or reproduced in any form by print,
photoprint, microfilm, or any other means, without written permission from the
publishers*

ISBN 90 279 3281 6

Printed in The Netherlands by Mouton & Co., The Hague

TO MY WIFE
Dorothy Rhode
Sine qua non

MAR 17 76

HUNT LIBRARY
CARNEGIE-MELLON UNIVERSITY

PREFACE

Literary historians of the American local color movement (1865-1900), both contemporary and more recent, have offered various explanations for the rise of this peculiar phenomenon and various judgments regarding its literary significance. Although the movement was first identified nearly a century ago, there has not been, until recently, much sifting and analyzing of its literary content by serious scholars, with the single exception of Fred Lewis Pattee, whose *American Literature Since 1870* appeared in 1916. Among the authors commonly associated with the movement, one stands apart from the rest – Mark Twain, whose clear genius seemed destined to overflow the local color mold and to establish him as a center of critical acclaim for work done without, as well as within, the local color tradition.

By 1900, when the American reading public had become bored with most of the lush output of local magazine fiction, the term "local color" had acquired a pejorative meaning. Thus it is not surprising that much of the literature to which the term applied remained, at least for the first several decades of the Twentieth Century, well beneath the level of scholarly attention.

At the present time a revival of interest on the part of scholars as well as readers seems to be in the making. New editions and collections of local color stories are being published, as well as numerous biographical and critical studies of individual authors. Whether this interest springs from neo-Romanticism, neo-Primitivism, anti-urbanism, ecological idealism, or some other form of spiritual yearning, one hesitates to say. Yet it is evident that a practically "lost" generation of American authors is being recovered for the present-day reader.

This book, based upon a review of the short fiction of representative figures of the movement, and of many of the contemporary and recent pronouncements applied to them, is not intended to be comprehensive; it merely suggests the possibility of a different way of viewing the whole body of local color literature, of a different way of assessing its significance in American literary history.

Gratitude is expressed to Professor Theodore Hornberger for having directed, at the University of Texas, my doctoral research upon which this work is based; to Texas A&I University for a research grant to defray expenses incurred in the preparation of the manuscript; to the publishers of *College English* and *Colby Library Quarterly* for permission to reprint, in Chapters I and IV respectively, brief portions of articles previously published in their pages; and to Mrs. Ruth Word for her patient work as typist and proofreader.

Robert D. Rhode
Texas A&I University

CONTENTS

Preface 5

1. Introduction: Approach, Definitions, and the Regional
   Factor 9

2. Setting as Background and Ornament 38

3. Setting in Close Relation to Character 82

4. Setting Personified 136

5. Conclusion 166

Bibliography 174

Index 185

TO MY WIFE
Sine qua non

1

INTRODUCTION: APPROACH, DEFINITIONS, AND THE REGIONAL FACTOR

APPROACH

This study will deal with the literature of one important phase of the history of American fiction during the latter part of the Nineteenth Century. That phase, commonly referred to as "the local color movement", found its expression mainly in a new fictional form, the modern American short story with an emphasis on setting. Whitman's glorious prophecy that all of the regions of America would voice the essences of their localities in a cooperative nationalism did achieve a degree of fulfillment in the local color fiction from 1865-1900. The abundance of land and the variety of topographical and climatic conditions in this country have perhaps made American authors as a whole more conscious of their outdoor physical surroundings than European writers.[1] This interest was clearly evident in the work of the American frontier humorists in the decades before the Civil War. And, as might be expected, the War itself brought on an increasing awareness of landscape and scenery as a result of a number of large-scale shifts in population, exposing new regions to closer observation.

We must not assume, however, that the popular interest in landscapes was a wholly autochthonous element in Amercian literature. That this interest had important European antecedents is beyond question; yet it drew much of its inspiration from the unique social and topographical conditions prevailing in rural America just after the Civil War. Conditions were then so favorable in American

[1] Cf. Louis Wann, *The Rise of Realism: American Literature from 1860 to 1888* (New York, 1937), 2.

soil that minor transplants from European fiction produced in America a massive florescence that dominated our literary destiny for a full generation. The American genre of local color possessed a confident, patriotic, national spirit, as historican A. H. Quinn observes:

After the war, which preserved the Union, it seemed as though fiction had a mission to portray all sections of the reunited country to each other and by interpreting the racial strains which made up the United States provide that understanding which would make possible the "more perfect union" of which the founders of the Republic had dreamed. It seems at first glance a paradox that the emphasis upon local color should tend toward a solidarity of feeling, but to those who realize that the strength of the Union depends upon the freedom of each section to govern its own local affairs, there is no paradox.[2]

The scope of this study of setting in the story of local color will not include all of the post-Civil-War fiction of America. "It would obviously be impossible," Quinn tells us, "even to chronicle all the fiction, especially the short stories, which from 1870 on capitalized on this interest"[3] in local areas. Since some restriction, even though arbitrary, must be made, it has been thought best to concentrate upon one literary type – the short story – clearly the foremost vehicle in both quality and quantity. Carl Van Doren goes so far as to say of Harte and his followers that when they attempted longer patterns, they "did little more than expand short stories or string them together on a casual thread; and that the history of local color must be left primarily to the historian of the short story".[4] Occasionally it will be desirable to make use of some of the more important novels and novelettes, though the short story alone exhibits most of the significant aspects of the American local color movement. One other restriction has been found necessary: only the ten chief figures in the localized story, representing four great geographical areas in America, have been given individual treatment. Harte and Twain represent the Far West; Cable, Murfree, Page and Allen represent the South; Jewett and Freeman represent New England; and Eggleston and Garland represent the Middle

---

[2] *American Fiction, An Historical and Critical Survey* (New York, 1936), 373.
[3] Idem.
[4] *The American Novel*, revised and enlarged (New York, 1940), 203.

West. Almost every conceivable use of the American scene appears in the works of these prime artists.

During the period 1865-1900 the short story was not only the most popular narrative vehicle, but was also the principal focus of experimentation in widely scattered parts of America. The local color movement in an intellectual sense can be viewed either as an effect, or, and perhaps more wisely, as an aspect of various philosophical, scientific, and cultural developments in the intellectual activity of the nation. For the purpose of definition and clarification, some of these broader matters must be briefly touched upon in this introductory chapter before the analysis of the techniques of individual authors can begin.

Before proceeding to definitions, however, a word needs to be said in justification of the unusual approach in this study. A good deal of competent writing about the local colorists has been done by biographers, historians, critics, and anthologists. Various aspects of the fiction of the period have been treated. But curiously, very meager attention has been given to the analysis of setting functions in local color fiction, clearly the chief and the most distinctive element in local color fiction.

The chief historian of the fiction of this period, Fred Lewis Pattee,[5] has made enlightening comments upon the treatment of setting by various individual writers, but his estimates have been more broadly critical than analytical and comprehensive. V. L. Parrington's[6] work in this period remains incomplete, unfortunately, and the completed sections deal with the literary use of backgrounds only in a very general way. The history of American fiction by A. H. Quinn gives relatively little attention to this phase of the local color movement, usually merely identifying the particular authors with the regions to which they belong and commenting upon the general point of view from which they worked. Other historians and anthologists of the period, such as Granville Hicks,[7]

---

[5] *The Development of the American Short Story, An Historical Survey* (New York and London, 1923), and *A History of American Literature Since 1870* (New York, 1916). Hereafter these studies will be designated as *American Short Story* and *American Literature Since 1870*.

[6] *The Beginnings of Critical Realism in America, 1860-1920* (New York, 1930).

[7] *The Great Tradition, An Interpretation of American Literature Since the Civil War* (New York, 1935).

Louis Wann, Harry R. Warfel,[8] and Claude M. Simpson,[9] are much interested in the local color movement, but as yet no one has seen fit to analyze the mass of localized stories from the standpoint of setting.[10]

This present study, by concentrating upon this significant aspect, aims to advance a step beyond the previous investigations in this field. For the sake of simplicity, all setting functions will be grouped under three main headings: Setting as Background and Ornament, Setting in Close Relation to Character, and Setting Personified. These headings will serve as titles for the three main chapters of this study.

DEFINITIONS

It is of course impossible to define the terms used in this book in a way that will be satisfactory to all; a reasonable clarity and consistency are all that should be attempted. Since some of the important expressions, such as *local color*, *setting*, the *short story*, etc., are terms with a history, it will be necessary to show how some of the concepts have arisen. Though there has not been much change of meaning in these terms since 1900, the definitions of that date are preferred in this study to those of the current usage. A literary movement is not properly viewed as an absolute phenomenon; it is what the past and the present have conceived it to be.

Local Color

Originally applied only to painting, the term *local color* was used in English as early as 1721 to mean "that colour which is natural to each object or part of a picture independently of the general

---

[8] With G. Harrison Orians, *American Local Color Stories* (New York, 1941).

[9] Claude M. Simpson, *The Local Colorists: American Short Stories, 1857-1900* (New York, 1960).

[10] Elias Lieberman, *The American Short Story, A Study of the Influence of Locality on its Development* (Ridgewood, New Jersey, 1912), might be regarded as an exception. This early short work, however, merely points up the importance of approaching the study of fiction from the standpoint of locality.

colour-scheme of the distribution of light and shade".[11] But out of the confusion that often arises when a critical term is shifted from one realm of art to another, the expression came by 1884 to denote, with reference to literature, "the representation in vivid detail of the characteristic features of a particular period or country (e.g. manners, dress, scenery, etc.), in order to produce an impression of actuality".[12] For some authors and critics, perhaps a majority, local color has meant not so much a method of accuracy and detail in the representation of any scene, as a search for novelty in a carefully isolated and therefore quaint corner of the world. Though the critics of the eighties, nineties, and later generally agreed on the books which would pass as local color literature, their definitions and analyses of this doubtful element remained throughout the period a subject of no little controversy and confusion.

Much of that confusion the English and American writers inherited along with the phrase from the French novelists of the eighteen-twenties and thirties. Théophile Gautier, for whom *la couleur locale* was a watch word and a Holy Grail, seems to have initiated a vogue which later drew in such disciples as Mérimée, Loti, and Nerval. "The cry for local color [in France] was the cry of revolt against this tyrannous uniformity", writes a later American critic; "a cry for the concrete and the characteristic in place of the conventional type."[13] This demand was clear enough, but history shows that there were almost as many ideas about how color should be attained as there were significant authors in France. Saint-Pierre and Hugo took the road to exoticism and orientalism; Balzac, Gautier, and Chateaubriand followed Rousseau's cult of scenery worship; Flaubert and Mérimée, in their maturity, turned to the more accurate objective method of positive science; and finally Zola taught his group the use of realistic-naturalistic "documents".

As already intimated, the only element which all of these approaches had in common – and they have all had some weight in determining the character of the American school – was a uniform

---

[11] *The New English Dictionary*, VI, 379-80.
[12] Idem.
[13] W. P. James, "On the Theory and Practice of Local Color", *Living Age*, CCXIII, 746 (June 12, 1897).

HUNT LIBRARY
CARNEGIE-MELLON UNIVERSITY

tendency, a gift of the scientific spirit, to lay stress on the background, the milieu, the atmosphere, the environment, the setting.
One reason for the absence of a wholly satisfactory definition of
local color is perhaps the fact that the earlier critics conceived of
it entirely in terms of romanticism and realism. However useful
these terms may be for some literary aspects of the period, they
are almost worthless when applied to local color. On the one hand
local color is fundamentally romantic, occupying itself with the
strange, the remote, the picturesque, the unfamiliar in place and
time; on the other hand it is fundamentally realistic, preferring the
immediate, the minute, the familiar, the scrupulously authentic.[14]
The wildest imagination and the scientific data sheet may both be
legitimate sources for its literary material. Nevertheless, most
scholars who have written about the movement have defined it
almost entirely in terms of romanticism and realism, generally as a
sort of vague transitional stage between the two, between Victorian
romanticism and twentieth century realism.[15] There is an abundance of critical opinion, however, that seems to deny this conception, including references to the existence of a more or less conscious and rather well-unified movement with its own critics and
disciples.

Another argument against a definition of local color purely in
terms of romanticism and realism lies in the breadth of meaning
which the phrase soon came to acquire. A good definition of local
color must take into account such extremes as are represented in
the work of James Lane Allen and Hamlin Garland, both of whom
considered themselves local colorists and set down their creeds in
writing. Allen saw an opportunity to avoid the apparent confusion
in the idea of local color and to purify the movement by going
back toward the oldest meaning of the phrase. Color must be taken
to mean literally color. His exposition of the term may be quoted
from the *Critic* of 1886:

[14] Cf. ibid., 748.
[15] This is the view of Tremaine MacDowell in "Regionalism in American Literature", *Minnesota History*, XX, 105-18 (June, 1939). Later writers supporting this
definition are D. A. Dike, "Notes on Local Color and its Relation to Realism",
College English, XIV (November, 1952), 81-88; and R. M. Weaver, "Realism and
the Local Color Interlude", *Georgia Review*, XXII (Fall, 1968), 301-305.

One everywhere meets with this phrase in current criticism of fiction. It becomes important, therefore, to give it the anchor of an exact meaning, lest it be tossed hither and thither over the sea of speech until it be worthless.... It does not concern the novelist as a student of human life, but as an artist of pictorial environment and phenomena. It withdraws his attention from character, plot, incident, motive, and fixes it upon skies, atmospheres, horizons, landscapes, sites, monuments – everything in short, by which human life in the locality chosen is colored, illuminated or darkened. In truth, human life becomes to him a part of nature and must be depicted as such: and nature everywhere dresses in characteristic and faultless colors....[16]

To realize how literally the word *color* in the phrase *local color* was sometimes interpreted, it is only necessary to read from such a manifesto as that of S. Baring-Gould, an English local colorist:

In story-writing it is always well, I may say almost essential, to see your scenes in your mind's eye, and to make of them pictures, so that your figures group and pose, artistically but naturally, and that there shall be colour introduced. The reader has thus a pleasant picture presented to his imagination. In one of my stories I sketched a girl in a white frock leaning against a sunny garden wall, tossing guelder roses. I had some burnished gold-green flies on the old wall, preening in the sun; so, to complete the scene, I put her on gold-green leather shoes, and made the girl's eyes of much the same hue. Thus we had a picture where the colour was carried through, and, if painted, would have been artistic and satisfying. A red sash would have spoiled all, so I gave her one that was green. So we had the white dress, the guelder-rose balls greeny-white, and through the ranges of green-gold were led up to her hair, which was red-gold.[17]

A wholly different effort was made to clarify the phrase and end its ambiguity by offering an extremely broad definition which would easily include everything alleged to be local color. Garland no doubt had this purpose in mind, though he was at the same time desirous of restoring the term to literary repute. Thus with Garland local color became synonymous with almost everything vital and interesting in literature; it was with Whitmanesque optimism that he stated the case of his school in the past, present, and future:

Local color in fiction is demonstrably the life of fiction. It is the native element, the differentiating element. It corresponds to the endless and vital charm of individual peculiarity.

[16] "Local Color", *The Critic*, VIII, 13 (January 9, 1886).
[17] "Color in Composition", *On the Art of Writing Fiction* (London, 1894), 35-46.

Historically, the local color of a poet or dramatist is of greatest value. The charm of Horace is the side light he throws on the manners and customs of his time. The vital Homer lies, after all, in his local color, not in his abstractions.... Similarly, it is the local color of Chaucer that interests us today. Wherever the man of the past in literature showed us what he really lived and loved, he moves us.... Historically, local color has gained in beauty and suggestiveness and humanity from Chaucer down to the present day.... Every great moving literature is full of local color.

Today we have in America, at least, a group of writers who have no suspicion of imitation laid upon them. Whatever faults they may be supposed to have, they are at any rate, themselves.

Local color – what is it? It means that the writer spontaneously reflects the life which goes on around him. It is natural and unrestrained art.

As the reader will see, I am using local color to mean something more than a forced study of the picturesque scenery of a State.

Local color in a novel means that it has such quality of texture and back-ground that it could not have been written in any other place or by any one else than a native.

It means that the picturesque shall not be seen by the author....

And so in the novel, in the short story, and in the drama – by the work of a multitude of loving artists, not by the work of an over-topping personality – will the intimate social, individual life of the nation be depicted. Before this localism shall pass away, such a study will have been made of this land and people as has never been made by any other age or social group, – a literature from the plain people, reflecting their unrestrained outlook on life, subtle in speech and color, humane beyond precedent, humorous, varied, simple in means, lucid as water, searching as sunlight![18]

Garland was not alone in assigning such breadth of meaning to the term "local color", though few critics who agreed with him in this respect were so kindly disposed. Far more common was the tendency to use the term in a pejorative sense, to make local color the equivalent of everything artificial and degrading in the literature of the period, in short to identify it with its weakest aspects. In their indiscriminating disapprobation of local color, the reactionary critics seem to lump under that heading such widely variant defects as over-decorative background, exaggerated atmosphere, absurd fastidiousness in all details, superficiality in character treatment, lack of perspective in narrative art, and even a digressive and sentimental style. Some of the more reasonable critics admitted the possibility of a legitimate use of local color so

---

[18] "Local Color in Art", *Crumbling Idols* (Chicago, 1894), 57-68.

long as it did not attract the reader's attention to itself and thus violate the singleness of effect in the story. But more often the criticism was of a sweeping kind, as a single quotation will illustrate:

We all know to our sorrow what local color is. The novel of today reeks with it – dialects so carefully spelled as to be unintelligible, passages of precise description of persons and places, meticulous attention to costumes, forms, and customs. It is realism run mad....

The realist of this year of grace has fallen into the same delusion as the stage-managers, that elaborate and historically accurate setting is essential. But if the characterization be vital and the tale compelling in interest, the rest is leather and prunella.... Learn to distinguish between the essence and the accidents.[19]

More recent literary historians, though fully aware of the wide range of implications the term "local color" has acquired, have begun to see some new positive significance in the American local color stories. Alexander Cowie, though well aware of the shortcomings of the local color writers, notes a "seriousness", "an integrity", and "a finely poetic quality in their descriptions", in addition to their "honestly derived" and "authentic" characters.[20] Richard M. Weaver credits the movement with "the real beginning of aesthetic sensibility in America".[21]

As would be expected, most definitions of local color, like that of the *New English Dictionary*, fall safely between those of Allen and Garland. But all assume a literary objective which aims primarily at the interpretation of the American scene or landscape rather than at the revelation of universal truth or general laws of human nature. In philosophical terms, the literature of local color is one of Aristotelian particulars rather than Platonic forms.

As used in this book, then, *local color* will connote in itself neither approbation nor disapprobation; it will refer to those details in a narrative setting which particularize it in time and place. To the extent that the elements of fiction are mutually inclusive, local color has to do with character and plot, but its chief business is with setting, in relation to which it stands either as an auxiliary or

---

[19] "Worship of Local Color", *The Nation*, LXXXIV, 75 (January 24, 1907).
[20] *Rise of the American Novel* (New York, 1948), 536-37.
[21] Op. cit., 305.

as a component part. If successfully used, local color strengthens the setting by adding to the impression of actuality, and by so doing adds to the total effect of the story. As we shall see later, the degree of emphasis which it can sustain depends largely on the functions it has in the story, or the type of story in which it is used. Generally only a story of setting can bear a major use of local color.

Setting[22]

The setting of a story is usually defined as "the literary framework of a narrative of other composition",[23] or "the temporal and spatial environment of the action of a narrative".[24] H. B. Lathrop includes under the term "all the circumstances, material and immaterial, which surround the action and determine the conditions under which it takes place".[25] Bliss Perry considers it

as synonymous with milieu, – the circumstances, namely, that surround and condition the appearance of the characters. Sometimes the setting of a novel corresponds precisely to the scenic effects of the stage, in that it gives a mere background for the vivid presentation of the characters. It will thus be seen that in the setting, that *tertium quid* is something corresponding to "atmosphere" if we were to speak in terms of art, or "environment" if we were to use the terminology of science.[26]

According to Perry, the realization of the importance of setting, as well as the discovery of the various roles it may play in the story, is comparatively recent. Defoe, despite his "realism", never knew the power of settings; Fielding occasionally used scenery without lending it any real significance. It was not until the rise of the romantic movement at the close of the eighteenth century that setting began to have any real function in fiction. Anne Radcliffe was one of the first to give emotional significance to landscape. Among the significant English novelists of the nineteenth century

---

[22] A portion of this section, as well as a portion of the section on setting and natural scenery, appeared in an article, "Scenery and Setting: A Note on American Local Color", *College English*, XIII (November, 1951), 142-46.

[23] *The New English Dictionary*, VIII, 554.

[24] *Webster's New International Dictionary*, Second Edition, 2293.

[25] *The Art of the Novelist* (New York, 1919), 198.

[26] *A Study of Prose Fiction* (New York, 1920), 155.

the conscious and important use of setting advanced particularly with the work of Dickens, Eliot, and Hardy. This development was to some extent a reflection of a changing attitude throughout the world toward nature and natural scenery.[27]

One important factor that favored an interest in setting was the preoccupation with natural science. The impact of science upon literature produced, among other things, a naturalistic style of fiction. Zola and de Maupassant wrote fiction making use of the characteristic rather than the beautiful. Man was pictured as an atom in an orderly but indifferent world; nature and institutions were inconsiderate of his ambitions, his labors, his sufferings. There was no sympathetic relation between the individual and his environment, no teleological principle at work in the universe.

The desire of the artists to be faithful to their subjects led to a method of precise observation and objective presentation. Hence the renowned notebook of the local colorist, the individualized landscape, and the detailed literary document. The importance of background, or setting, to the naturalist needs scarcely to be mentioned. He was not so much an artist as a laboratory technician preparing a detailed report. The character in a story, his environment, and his specific reactions are all presented as parts of a sociological process.

In the fusion of these elements in the naturalistic story, character tends to suffer most, for, as man becomes a pawn in the hands of superior forces, he surrenders his individuality. Action becomes involuntary and therefore unheroic. Setting, however, tends to gain in importance. The landscapes and institutions, as objects of environment, become the prime movers, the cores of ethical, and therefore human, interest.

The crux of the problem of setting seems to be the relationship which setting as an art bears to the world of experience. Since it is generally conceded that all literature is based ultimately upon reality, its subject matter is necessarily drawn from the author's observation or vicarious experience, however arbitrarily selected or seriously altered in memory or imagination.

[27] Ibid., 163-66.

The local colorists after the Civil War, the setting specialists, desired as little rearrangement and distortion as possible. Most preferred to write with an eye on the object so as to subvert, as far as possible, the subjective factor of memory. But they faced a serious limitation: the weight of tradition surrounding man's relation to nature. If they hoped to see nature with the eyes of Homer, they failed, just as many others after Homer had failed. Rousseau's *Nouvelle Heloise*, published in 1761, is said to mark the beginning of the modern "romantic" love of scenery, though any such claim will obviously be viewed with skepticism.

During the period covered in this book, setting as a narrative element was still undergoing development in the American story. By 1900 almost all of the more general functions of setting had been discovered and each artist had his own special techniques and skills. The scheme by which these special techniques will be classified in this study provides three main headings: (1) Setting as Background and Ornament, including all purely decorative, incidental, or relatively independent types; (2) Setting in Close Relation to Character, including all types of environmental influence, parallelism between characters and setting, and symbolism through external scenes; and (3) Setting Personified, including all attempts to elevate an object, a general scene, a simple form of life, or nature in general, to a level of human-like animation or consciousness, and to make it function to some extent as a character in a story.

Setting and the Short Story Form

Historians have pointed out several causes for the replacement of the English serial by the American short story during the closing decades of the last century. The lack of an international copyright law before 1890 forced American writers of fiction to offer their products in competition with free British books. The market for novels was thereby sharply limited. The problem of adapting the novel to the American magazine, however, allowed a good deal of space for short pieces, for which there was a regular demand, provided the stories were written so as to appeal mainly to local interests. The maturity of the short story in America during this period led to its recognition in many quarters as America's own, though perhaps unique, contribution to the literary genres of the world. Irving, Hawthorne, and Poe had made a notable beginning, and the form was systematically, if somewhat arbitrarily, defined and registered in our literary history by Brander Matthews in his famous study[28] of 1884, the year which Pattee later referred to as "the climactic year of the short story in America".[29]

In specifying the form of the "short story" and in defining it to exclude the novel and the sketch, Matthews deals chiefly with its plot requirement, which he regards as its prime element and most distinctive feature. In the short story, he insists repeatedly, "something always happens". Though Zola may choose for his future novels "*une histoire quelconque*, any kind of a story, and make it serve his purpose, – which is to give elaborate pictures of life in all its minute details" – such a concept is entirely "a negation of the short-story".[30]

But the strict discipline which Matthews set for the short story was never taken seriously by the editors and authors themselves, least of all by the local colorists. By the end of the century, at any rate, its form was perhaps even less settled than that of the novel; almost anything, in fact, could pass as a short story. Reporting in 1898, Frederick Wedmore declared that the short story

may be an episode,... a fairy tale,... the presentation of a single character with the stage to himself..., a tale of the uncanny..., a dialogue of comedy..., a panorama of selected landscape, a vision of the sordid street, a record of heroism, a remote tradition or an old belief vitalized by its bearing on our lives to-day, an analysis of an obscure calling, a glimpse at a forgotten quarter.[31]

Of these casually listed potentialities, it will be noted that at least half suggest stories of setting and local color. Plot has been

---

[28] Matthews' definition first appeared anonymously in the *Saturday Review*, London, in the summer of 1884. It was reprinted in *Lippincott's Magazine* for October, 1885, and still later in his volume *Pen and Ink*, published in 1888. See his prefatory note to *The Philosophy of the Short Story* (New York, 1917).
[29] F. L. Pattee, "The Short Story", in *Cambridge History of American Literature*, III (New York, 1918), 388.
[30] Op. cit., 33.
[31] "The Short Story", *Littel's Living Age*, CCXVII, 397 (May 7, 1898).

pushed considerably to the rear. In fact, Wedmore states that by a short story, "I mean a short imaginative work in the difficult medium of prose; for plot, or story proper, is no essential part of it."[32]

Though there is yet some difference of opinion concerning the definition of the short story, there will be no difficulty, for the purposes of this study, in admitting as short stories all brief prose fiction which editors and literary historians have recognized as such. But the mere brevity of the short story, whatever its special character otherwise, presents a special problem in setting. The need of "working in" a whole story in a few thousand words obviously requires the elimination of all matter not absolutely vital to the story. This means that setting should ordinarily not be used merely to prepare a reader for an incident; it should be used rather sparingly as background.

Thus from one point of view, setting might appear to suffer more restriction than its coordinates. Yet the other elements are also restricted in special ways. Character, for instance, must usually remain static in the short story and incapable of growth as in the longer forms. But from another point of view the restrictions of space have had a wholesome effect upon the development of setting techniques in the short story. To quote again from Wedmore,

the very obligations of the short story are an advantage to its art. Nature in fiction requires to be seen, not in endless detail, as a botanical or geographical study, but, as in classic landscape composition, a noble glimpse of it over a man's shoulder, under a man's arm.[33]

Not only should description, if used at all, be well distributed throughout the short story, but other devices for setting should be rigidly economical and thoroughly efficient.

Aside from the brevity and economy of the short story, there is another feature of the type which conditions the use of setting within it. Whatever subject it may have is likely to be specialized and intense. Its scope is relatively limited, and it is more likely than the novel to conform to the classical unities. Were it not that time and place are relatively constant in the short story, local color stories would be well-nigh impossible. The short story is

---

[32] Ibid., 393.
[33] Ibid., 397.

also likely to tax the imagination more heavily because it must advance rapidly to a high peak of interest. Details must be used for great effectiveness, and for more than one purpose. Though separate passages may be devoted to the development of character, plot, and setting in the long narrative, it is practically essential that every passage in the short story contribute materially to all of the main elements simultaneously. For this reason it will be difficult to demonstrate by particular quotations the special functions of setting in some of the stories to be treated.

Another special feature of the short story that bears upon the use of setting is the great variety it exhibits with respect to the relative importance of character, setting, and plot. More than the novel, the short story seems to invite concentration upon one element. As already indicated, the earlier American short story as discussed by Matthews was mainly preoccupied with plot. The twentieth century story is chiefly character – "find the character and then get this story" is the slogan today. The story of the late nineteenth century may, as we shall see, be termed the story of setting. Writing in the *Atlantic* in 1902, Bliss Perry admitted the success of the setting specialists:

The nature of the short story is such that both characters and actions may be almost without significance, provided the atmosphere – the place and time – the background – is artistically portrayed.... The modern feeling for landscape, the modern curiosity about social conditions, the modern aesthetic sense as such, all play into the short story writer's hands. Many a reader, no doubt, takes up Miss Wilkins' stories, not because he cares much about the people in them or what the people do, but just to breathe for twenty minutes the New England air! You may even have home-sickness for a place you have never seen – some Delectable Duchy in Cornwall, a window in Thrums, a California mining camp deserted before you were born, – and Mr. Quiller Couch, or Mr. Barrie, or Bret Harte will take you there, and that is all you ask of them. The popularity which Stephen Crane's war stories enjoyed for a season was certainly not due to his characters, for his personages had no character, not even names, – nor to the plot, for there was none. But the sights and sounds and odors and colors of war – as Crane imagined war – were plastered upon his vacant-minded heroes as you would stick a poster to a wall, and the trick was done. In other words, the setting was sufficient to produce the intended effect.[34]

[34] "The Short Story", *Atlantic Monthly*, XC, 246 (August, 1902).

As this opinion indicates, there can be little doubt that by the end of the century the short story of setting had become a reality.

Setting and Natural Scenery

Another problem to be considered is that of the relationship which setting bears to those objects of the physical world which constitute our environment. The terms *scenery, natural scenery, nature,* and *landscape,* all of which are frequent in American literary criticism of the seventies and eighties, usually refer to the vast, the spectacular and relatively unchanged features in the topography of the country rather than to those which are the result of man's labor or planning. Man's clothing and bodily ornaments, the implements with which he works, to some extent his household furnishings, and even his dwelling itself, help to identify a place, but these features are commonly associated with his person rather than with the "nature" which surrounded him. The difficulty in science of drawing a clear distinction between man and his environment finds a parallel in the problem of distinguishing setting from character.

In the handling of natural scenery in fiction, one of the most difficult problems is that concerning "human interest". By the end of the century most critics believed that scenery in fiction arouses an interest only through association with human beings:

> Let the author's style be never so rich and brilliant, let him lay hold upon the choicest hidden beauties of the language and adorn his page with images of the most gorgeous or the most pathetic beauty; yet will the whole lack point and application and remain a dead impassive thing, until the *human figure* comes into relief – when the pulse of the reader leaps, the spell is woven, the interest is born.[35]

> The print apron of one cottage girl...is more important...to any novelist than the wildest heave of boulder-strewn moor or forest. Is it not a mistake ...to entitle a story by its setting and to introduce that setting with the utmost power and volume of words? ...We are not interested in such effects until the people interest us. The environment is important only as bringing out human nature in little unaccustomed ways.[36]

[35] Homer Clyde House, *A Theory of the Genetic Basis of Appeal in Literature* (Lincoln, Nebraska, n.d.), 50-51.
[36] "Scenery in Fiction", *Living Age*, CCXXXV, 813 (December 27, 1902).

Man is perennially interesting to man; nature is so only when man relates himself to her, puts purpose or meaning into her.[37]

The solution of this problem of whether an anti-social or a purely aesthetic interest in scenery is possible depends upon one's aesthetic theory. But at least four different affirmative positions have been suggested. First, there is the conception that man's emotional response to nature is an expression of his essential religious nature. One of its advocates, John Addington Symonds,[38] believes "it is an error to suppose that the ancients were insensible to the charm and beauty of external nature", though their sympathy with nature was anthropomorphic rather than romantic. During the Middle Ages, he continues, Christianity banished the deities and demigods from the earth and left man "face to face with a supreme abstraction, God", who became the sole reality. "All else was illusion, mirage, depending on the divine caprice." In more recent times nature became recognized as an oracle of God, through which great truths are revealed to man, and also as something kindred to himself, because divinely created.

This tendency to connect man's reaction to landscapes with his religious feelings was very common throughout the past century. It has become such a strong convention, writes T. H. Ferril,[39] that it often "thwarts the poet and causes him to waste time". The explanation which he offers is that a vast and spectacular scene calls back within the imagination of the author a primitive feeling of awe and wonder which leads him to use weak abstractions rather than vigorous details, and therefore to fail in concreteness. In fiction, he explains,

the same forces of mountain mysticism are at work. In abandoning the play for the setting the fiction writer feels under pressure to fit his characters to the vast panorama his eyes behold. He becomes oblivious of the complexities of natural experience and naively rationalizes history to select the most active behavior appropriate to the scene. This results in a simplifica-

---

[37] Norman Foerster, "Clerks of the Woods", *Nation*, XCVII, 120 (August 7, 1913).
[38] "Landscape", *Essays Speculative and Suggestive* (London, 1907), 269.
[39] "Writing in the Rockies; Religious Impulse, or Mysticism, Excited by Landscape", *Saturday Review of Literature*, XV, 3 (March 20, 1937).

tion of life into rather pure and tight patterns rigidly conventionalized. He continues heroes and heroines capable of meeting an apparent nature on its most elemental terms.

In a word Ferril asserts that no modern writer is free enough from feelings of awe and impotence in the presence of raw landscape to be able to use the scene in a credible story. "Low-grade animism" or "mysticism" permeates modern experience and precludes the possibility of a great story set in a magnificent mountainous region or a vast desert. Thus Ferril's position is not that nature is lacking in interest, but that it is too exciting to be safely used in fiction.

Many late nineteenth century critics, like the scientists, were inclined to connect the feeling for nature with practical utility. The popularity of emergent and cosmic evolution is reflected in a theory formulated by H. C. House.[40] The emotional reactions "which constitute the interest of literature", he believes, were "at some time in race history... a factor in survival". All aesthetic responses, whether first hand or vicarious, are explainable in terms of "natural selection". This would mean that man's present attitude toward nature has evolved as a selective characteristic, that his interest is deeply grounded and inseparable from the roots of his personality.

A third possibility, a thoroughly economic interpretation of man's emotional response to natural scenery, has been suggested by Havelock Ellis.[41] Though Ellis does not deny such anti-social values in a landscape as freedom from oppression and opportunity for relaxation, he subordinates them to economic values from which he believes they are derived by association. He cites the case of the medieval monks who built their monasteries in picturesque parts of the wilderness in an age when love of scenery was at its lowest ebb in history: "The spots they secured were not only cheap in hard cash because despised, and secluded because often situated among the hills, but they had the further advantage of being well wooded and that a stream ran through their midst."

Besides the religious, evolutionary, and economic interpretations

[40] Op. cit., 5.
[41] "Love of Wild Nature", *Contemporary Review*, XCV, 180-99 (February, 1909).

of man's aesthetic response to natural scenery, there was a mechanistic or purely physical one. Though suggestions of it appear in
late nineteenth century aesthetics, it is perhaps best stated in a
study made in 1912 by Walter B. Pitkin.[42] Despite the fact that
there are about four or five thousand smells, at least thirty-six
thousand colors, and countless other sensory perceptions that are
distinguishable in human experience, the differences in quality are
always slight. "All the pleasant impressions resemble one another
in some underlying characteristic in which a simple animal joy
predominates, while all the unpleasant seem merely so many sha-
dings of three things: panic, temperature, color feelings." One can
"pass from the joy of a noontide landscape to the melancholy of
a sunset simply by reducing the amount of light that falls upon the
scene... The range of atmospheric effects is slight". Thus in moods
brought on by natural scenes "there seems to be nothing more
than a little understood chemical process with certain light waves,
air pressure, and temperatures set up in the nervous system". It
is "probably the merest coincidence that some of the feelings caused
by these chemisms closely resemble those associated with certain
thoughts". Where there is a resemblance, an author may use setting and character to intensify each other. He may work from
two independent sources and still be able to achieve a single emotional effect.

Regardless of the truth concerning the source of feelings for
nature, they must be recognized as something more than literary
conventions or habits. James Lane Allen's stories, for example,
show a passion for trees and birds reminiscent of animism, hylozoism, and other ancient mystic cults. Though such elements clash
with the Darwinian tone he sometimes assumes, they illustrate the
wide range which the local colorists used in their search for novel
uses of setting.

Regionalism, Local Tradition, and Atmosphere

Regionalism, a term often applied to local color literature, should be

---

[42] *The Art and Business of Story Writing* (New York, 1912).

distinguished from *sectionalism*, which refers usually to an aggressive, political, or patriotic interest in some part of the country and is propagandistic in tone. *Regionalism*, which is now applied mainly to a new movement of the present century, provides a legitimate subject matter for literature.[43] Donald Davidson has defined regional literature in part as "a self-conscious expression of the life of a region", which "may exploit intimate and local aspects of its scene, thus recovering the 'usable past' so much referred to".[44] If regionalism is to be defined, however, as Allen Tate defines it, as "only the immediate, organic sense of life in which a fine artist works",[45] it may hardly be distinguished from its nineteenth century prototype. Both movements produced literature pertaining to particular regions. The contemporary movement is generally recognized as an offspring of the local color movement, differing from its parents by greater depth and a superior sense of tradition. B. A. Botkin is striving at such a distinction when he says that

Regional coherences exist, to be cultivated by the artist, not for a peculiar glamour of picturesqueness or quaintness, ...but as a means to the end of social portraiture and the expression of personality with roots.[46]

Some of the local colorists undoubtedly neglected to give roots to their characters – they were bent on seeing life rather than knowing it. During their time the American scene was more heterogeneous than it is today, and particularization of character and scene was therefore possible by relatively superficial treatment. As significant distinctions became harder, either through nationalizing influences in the country or through an exhaustion of living models, the output was maintained only by the literary opportunist whose results became proportionately more artificial and trivial.

A few of the cleverest native authors learned a new way to individualize their material: by a literary use of tradition. Though tradition, as Tate has pointed out, has actually nothing to do with the past except for the historical fact of its origin somewhere in

---

[43] See Allen Tate, "Regionalism and Sectionalism", *New Republic*, LXIX, 158-61 (December 23, 1931).
[44] "Regionalism and Nationalism in American Literature", *American Review*, V, 53 (April, 1935).
[45] Tate, op. cit., 157.
[46] "Regionalism: Cult or Culture?" *English Journal*, XXV, 184 (March, 1936).

time,[47] a reader can be expected to know local conventions of only a few of the oldest sections of the country. For this reason a use of tradition comparable to that in Europe was out of the question. In a study entitled "The Background of the American Novel", Robert Herrick explained the situation as follows:

Another and much more important quality of our landscape, which makes it unyielding material for the imaginative artist, is its almost universal lack of high civilization. The marriage of man with the soil, so essential a feature of European countries, has with us been accomplished but recently, and has been frequently disturbed by successive, rapid economic changes, so that the marks of the union are scarcely evident or are already almost obliterated in many sections of the country. As one passes over the surface of Europe, no matter how hastily, one is aware of a human quality in the fields, the roads, the water courses, – above all in the kind of housing men have made for themselves on their soil. Here is a mother earth that has been lived upon by her children for generations; and through the forces of human contact after centuries of war and peace, birth and death and change, she has come to have an individual expression of her own, subtly reflecting the character of her human children. There is little of this sort of thing in the United States. The face of nature, no longer, alas! virginal, even in our far western States, has not yet achieved a distinct maturity, although the soil has been ploughed for a number of generations.... Man has camped upon the land, erecting temporary and incongruous structures in which to house himself and the instruments of his activity. He has worked the soil ruthlessly to get whatever there is in it or under it: he has not yet moulded its face to himself, – lived in the deeper sense with it.[48]

In a few regions of America, in the South and in the New England states, there was something of a local tradition, as will be seen in the stories of Cable, Page, and Freeman, but there was scarcely anything of the sort in the Middle or Far West. This was doubly unfortunate: in the first place, because of the absence in the newer regions of capable native authors, and, in the second place, because the literature of the older areas was destined to be domestic and effeminate. An editor of the *Nation* described the situation in 1919 thus:

As Americans were generally a nomadic people, any writer who wrote about a community long enough established to have manners of its own

---

[47] Op. cit., 160.
[48] "The Background of the American Novel", *Yale Review*, III, 221-23 (January, 1914).

had to write about the village concerns of that part of the population which had been too conservative – often too dull or timid – to move about over the country after the manner of the bolder spirits.[49]

Whether or not a considerable time element is required in order for a local tradition to emerge, there can be little doubt that time is essential for the author to become aware of it so that he can put it to creditable literary use. "Time is the essence of the undertaking," writes Mary Austin, "time to live in the land and absorb it; still more time to cure the reading public of its preference for something less than the proverbial bird's-eye view of the American scene."[50] There was a difference of opinion, quite naturally, as to whether it was essential for an author to be a native of a region in order to make use of its tradition. The real question was whether writing traditionally meant writing in a tradition or about a tradition. To write in a tradition, Allen Tate explains – and he believes this to be the only legitimate use of tradition in literature –

is to approach the chosen subject matter with an instinct for its meaning, rather than with an abstract theory about it or with an air of contriving for oneself all the properties of the scene.... A real tradition is individual, it is a special organization of the individual sensibility that liberates the intelligence through the possession of habitual responses to life that are, moreover, relevant to the conduct of other men.[51]

To write about a tradition, on the other hand, is to treat the uniformities of thought and action of a particular group from an external or objective point of view; they become subject matter rather than a characteristic of style. It is evident that the use of tradition in an objective or wholly conscious way requires a vast amount of literary skill, but is not, as Tate implies, an impossibility. To endow a scene with a convincing semblance of age and custom requires more than the cumulative force of concrete detail; the problem is that of creating an atmosphere.

Atmosphere has been defined as "the surrounding mental or moral element",[52] or "the process that creates the reader's mood

---

[49] "Local Color and After", *The Nation*, CIX, 427 (September 27, 1919).

[50] "Regionalism in American Fiction", *English Journal*, XXI, 107 (February, 1932).

[51] Op. cit., 159-60.

[52] *New English Dictionary*, I, 537.

and brings it into perfect accord with the story's setting".[53] Atmosphere is closely associated with setting as these definitions indicate; it refers usually to the mood or "humour" with which the physical setting is characterized, such as wonder, terror, or nostalgia. It is the *genius loci*, a quality which corresponds to what H. B. Lathrop means by "the spirit of the scene"; it is not the scene itself, "but a way of feeling about the scene".[54] Interpreted liberally it is also his "immaterial aspect of setting, ...the medium in which the characters live; the body of sentiments, ideas, customs, faiths; the civilization or culture of which the characters are a part; the 'milieu' of the story".[55]

THE REGIONAL FACTOR

The literature of the American local color movement is usually studied by large geographic areas, or regions and subregions, extending to virtually every geographic, cultural, and ethnic subdivision of the United States during the Post Civil War era of 1865-1900. Of the four major regions, the stories of the Far West held the national spotlight during the seventies, the South during the eighties, New England during the nineties, and the Middle West at the end of the century.

The short story produced in the Far West after the Civil War had been derived partly from the older literary tradition of Irving and Hawthorne, partly from the physical manner of life in the West, and partly from the personalities of those unusual men who write most perceptively of this large section, Bret Harte and Mark Twain. Their personal relationship, the influences which they directly or indirectly exerted on each other's work, and the similarity of the subject matter which they used, tended to make their work homogeneous. Both were writing for about the same set of readers, and were appealing to about the same emotions and curiosities. Both were in a sense expert journalists, covering with more or less reportorial thoroughness, if not altogether truthfully, the same vast assignment.

[53] H. A. Phillips, *Art in Short Story Narration* (New York, 1913), 97.
[54] Lathrop, op. cit., 222.
[55] Ibid., 223.

The Far West was indeed a vast, sparsely inhabited region, greatly varied in topography and climate, filled with danger and opportunity sufficient to stagger the imagination. To the successive waves of adventurers, miners, and home-seekers from back East, the land appeared raw and challenging. With them the indigenous Indian and early Spanish people and cultures did not count for much; when not threatening, these were ignored or treated with contempt. The older American immigrants themselves, however, were soon being absorbed into a new quick-growth, composite Western culture that was to become fascinating to tourists, reporters, and readers back home. By 1865 the mining camps exhibited a predominately male population with new codes and moral patterns adapted to their peculiar social and geographic environment. Desperadoes, rootless fortune-hunters and earnest home-seekers all showed remarkable ingenuity and humor in their struggle for survival. Naturally, the only local colorists available to exploit this new material were relatively recent immigrants themselves, subject to the limitations of an outsider's point of view. Hence the artificiality and superficiality usually attributed to the local color literature of the Far West.

Whereas the local color literature of the West had a hard, raw material, impressive by magnitude and abundance, that of the South derived its charm chiefly from temporal remoteness and cultural uniqueness. The South was the older region, though slower in developing literary self-consciousness. After the War the rapid influx of Northern attitudes and enterprises worked toward the banishment of the cultural gentility of the Old South along with its outmoded economic structure. But the Southern aesthetic temperament and sense of dignity, natural characteristics of a class maintained by a slavery economy, were not easily laid away.[56] Wounded and emotionally crushed, many survivors of the War generation had neither the flexibility nor the morale to adapt themselves to a new economy and theory of life; they lived out their lives proudly yet pathetically, impersonating the gentlemen

---

[56] See Parrington, *The Romantic Revolution in America* (New York, 1927), 3-125; also Granville Hicks, *The Great Tradition, an Interpretation of American Literature Since the Civil War* (New York, 1935), 1-3.

and ladies of their memories, spending their days in reminiscence in nostalgic reveries of a faded glory. For years after the War the very landscape in the deep South, the decaying white mansions with weed-infested rose gardens, the unrepaired fences and dilapidated sheds, the vast uncultivated fields, were, to the uprooted aristocracy, pathetic reminders of a happy long ago.

Because of its peculiar "landocracy" and the sparsity of its population, the South had long before the War developed a great variety of local traditions, especially in the mountains and in the damp and heavily wooded districts where there was little wealth or outside communication. Blood ties were strong, racial clannishness was prevalent, and strong local sentiments persisted within nearly every community that was topographically or culturally isolated. At the time of the War the Southern lands had been completely settled; the population was relatively stable and the percentage of recent emigres was small.

The educated minority should have been able to unite the divergent elements of ante-bellum culture to produce a regional literary tradition. Certain special conditions in the Old South, however, hindered the development of a literary school. To begin with, its intellectual tradition was ultra-conservative and rested in the hands of a class to whom literature was at best a hobby. Because of the prevalence of political ambition, an oratorical style was cherished above a natural manner of literary expression. Unfortunately oratorical flowers and Addisonian essays were out of fashion in the East, and the Old South had but few periodicals of its own. Furthermore, the Southern localities could not be easily reported by an outsider because there was little spectacle that could be adequately interpreted from the surface. To interpret the South a native was essential, for only a native could know intimately the roots of Southern culture or follow the labyrinthine growth of tradition. The literary exploitation of New England was facilitated by the nearness of publishers and markets; that of the Far West by the gold rush publicity and the immediate compelling power of the material itself; that of the South only by the publicity of the War plus the initiative taken by Eastern publishers. Thus chronologically the initiation of the Southern movement is relatively late, belonging chiefly to the eighties, whereas the Western and to some extent the Eastern belongs rather to the seventies.

From the Post-War generation, a generation familiar with modern trends but old enough to remember something of the times "befo' de wah", such writers as Cable, Page, Murfree, and Allen formed the color school of the South. These four have been selected to represent the South during this period, not so much because they were especially experimental in their settings, but because they best covered the divergent aspects of the Southern scene, and each produced at the highest literary level of his time.

As the story of the West coheres as a special type because of its vigor, mobility, irony and humor, the story of the South is marked by sentiment, nostalgia, and delicacy. "It needs but little imagination", said a critic in *The Nation* for August, 1888, "for a Southerner to tell a tale of hearts broken and homes laid waste."[57] As the Western story is set upon a background replete with optimistic excitement, sudden transformations, abundance, awesome magnitude, newness, rawness, and opulent beauty, the Southern story runs through a landscape that is characterized by decadent loveliness and mellow ripeness. The "heroic" tone of the West gives way to a plaintive, elegiac note, tragic with the solemn regret for a magnificence and gaiety that are no longer to be found.

In New England after the War a social picture prevailed which was vaguely similar to that of the South, yet almost a direct contrast to the social scene in the Far West. The men who were young and strong had departed in the successive waves of Western immigration, because their native section could offer them no real economic opportunity. The shipping trade had subsided, the farms were unproductive, and the textile mills offered only a meager wage for women and children. New England villages were losing their more vigorous and enterprising population to the areas whose resources were less fully exploited, so that the remaining inhabitants, F. O. Matthiessen tells us, were

old women and children, retired captains who had not seen a ship for thirty years, eccentric characters of all sorts driven by too much isolation

[57] *The Nation*, XLVII, 95 (August 2, 1888).

into humors and oddities, distorted old maids, and awkward girls over whose starved emotions already hung the shadow of a kindred distortion.[58]

In keeping with this picture, the writers who recorded the New England decline were practically all women. The literary men who did their best to carry on the illustrious poetic and intellectual tradition of the pre-war literary galaxy were Howells and Aldrich, both of whom, as Matthiessen points out, came from the outside. Two New England women, Sarah Orne Jewett and Mary E. Wilkins Freeman, stand out distinctly among the long list of native New England writers of the new generation who were old enough to know personally the survivors of the golden age, and who were young enough to have been influenced by the newer style of localized fiction. Harriet Beecher Stowe, already fifty at the outbreak of the war, gave a literary interpretation to early and middle nineteeth-century New England in her *Oldtown Folks* (1869) and *The Pearl of Orr's Island* (1862). Stowe's New England is the New England of burning issues, bold intellectual power and enterprise, of literary florescence. But the ebb-tide New England of Jewett and Freeman is a land marked by decay, old age, loneliness and frustration.

New England after the war had, like parts of the South, a glorious history and a relatively fixed tradition, but its features were not sufficiently unique or spectacular to afford such striking material as either the South or the Far West. Though Jewett's first New England stories appeared along with Harte's first successes, her reputation grew only very gradually. There was little violent drama or activity in the deserted New England towns to serve as a basis for long, "heroic" tales of dashing characters and complications. More feasible was the short narrative sketch, setting forth a particular moment or episode in the commonplace lives of simple, humble people. The New England short story, considered as a special type, tends to be therefore brief and almost formless, effeminate in technique, trivial in plot and action, but intimate and sincere in its manner and style.

The last of four great geographical areas to be considered in

[58] F. O. Matthiessen, "New England Stories", in *American Writers on American Literature*, ed. John Macy (New York, 1921), 400.

this study, the Middle West, shows a culture and tradition as varied as its topography. With each of the other three regions, which it adjoins both physically and culturally, it has something in common. The Middle West in the fifties had the religious scrupulosity of New England without its intellectual tradition; the coarseness and crime of the Far West without its mineral riches; the agricultural problems of the South without its slave economy or its social magnificence. After the war the Middle West offered perhaps the least opportunity for exciting literary materials, for there was nothing in its monotonous industry or its toilsome agriculture to appeal to the fancy of the genteel generation.

Even here, however, there was a place for an earnest historian who did not demand spectacle and color, and for a native artist who could sense in the back-breaking, soul-rending struggles of the people of this region something wholly fit for the highest artistic purposes. "It was on the frontier", Carl Van Doren believes,

that realism took its first definite stand. Perhaps some barrenness in the life of the Middle West, lacking both the longer memories of the Atlantic States and the splendid golden expectations of California, discouraged romance there and set going that tendency toward naturalism which descends unbroken from Edward Eggleston (1837-1902) through E. W. Howe and Hamlin Garland....[59]

The older Middle West is best seen in the homely Hoosier stories of Eggleston, the pioneer regionalist who could write truthfully and realistically of its slackness and drab poverty without neglecting its beauty and its variety. In his work, according to Parrington, "there was no brooding sense of social justice, of wrongs done the Middle Border by unjust laws"; but

In the year 1887...came a significant change of temper. Three very different writers – Harold Frederick, Joseph Kirkland, and Hamlin Garland – turned to the theme of farm life, and dealt with it in a mordantly realistic vein. It was the first conscious literary reaction to the subjection of Agriculture to capitalistic exploitation and it was marked by the bitterness of a decaying order.[60]

In the later group Hamlin Garland stands out both as the most

[59] Carl Van Doren, *The American Novel* (New York, 1921), 129-30.
[60] Parrington, *Critical Realism*, 288.

skillful writer of short stories and most significant local colorist in theory and practice. Eggleston and Garland, therefore, are chosen to represent the development of experiments with setting in the story of this section.

The local color story of the Middle West, in so far as it has an individuality of its own, may be described as frank, sometimes coarse, and altogether masculine. Aside from Mark Twain's few tales of the Far West, the Middle Western story is, in both form and content, perhaps the least indebted to older models and traditions of our entire literature of the period.

2

SETTING AS BACKGROUND AND ORNAMENT

This book, as previously stated, approaches American local color from the standpoint, not of its regional content, but of its literary method of utilizing this content. It is best to begin at the lowest level of setting utilization, that is, at the level of setting as background and ornament, in which all of the local colorists of the period are involved. Without exception, they employed ordinary scenic description to some degree, many to excess.

Bret Harte, a pioneer in the American short story of local color, had a predilection for the most spectacular and the picturesque, even in his earliest writings, and a tendency to affect the "heroic" in his landscapes. In "My Metamorphosis", which appeared in *The Golden Era* in April, 1860, he lays his initial scene in an English ancestral park esteemed for its charm; yet Harte's description is incredibly artificial, vague, and ineffectual:

The grounds were tastefully adorned; there were groups of statuary, and the never-failing Italian accessories of hills and fountains.... At length Mr. Willoughby, Ada, a few ladies and myself, seated ourselves by the margin of an artificial lake, from whose centre a trickling fountain sent its spray toward the clear blue sky. The evening was deliciously cool and Ada lent her sweet voice to the rippling water.[1]

The author's ignorance of the subject seems to have ruined him, as well as his lack of literary experience. In the same year, however, Harte was relatively successful with his descriptive art in "The Work on Red Mountain", his first Western story, though he was unable for the next eight years to duplicate this achievement. The

[1] *The Writings of Bret Harte*, 20 vols., Riverside edition (Boston and New York, c. 1910), XX (ed. C. M. Kozlay), 8-9.

stories collected by C. M. Koslay[2] representing Harte's uncollected work up to 1865, and those Western sketches and legends which appeared in the volume *Condensed Novels and Other Papers* first issued in 1867, have little merit, from any point of view, though in a number of them he attempts to portray the country later used in his best stories. Even Harte's enlarged revision of "The Work on Red Mountain" (*Golden Era*, December, 1860), his one successful story before 1868, was practically ignored. The difference between success and failure was due to something more than a choice of subject, or the use of a particular background. An argument can be made that it was the treatment, not the choice, of background material that made Harte's West sometimes palatable and sometimes unpalatable. It will be seen in the next chapter that Harte's best stories, especially those in *The Luck of Roaring Camp* collection, reflect a proper integration of setting with other story elements, an achievement consistently lacking in his inferior tales, in which he sometimes used his setting purely as background or ornament. The stories in which Harte did not even attempt to give his setting some vital connection with the other elements are fortunately few, for they were practically all failures.

One of the least objectionable of these is "The Idyll of Red Gulch" (*Overland*, December, 1869), which, like "The Luck of Roaring Camp" and "The Outcasts of Poker Flat", includes the name of a place in its title. Its setting, however, is actually no more than an ornamental stage. It is the account of a love affair of a school-mistress, an outsider, and a village drunkard who falls asleep under an azalea-bush:

Meanwhile the shadows of the pine-trees had slowly swung around until they crossed the road, and their trunks barred the open meadows with gigantic parallels of black and yellow. Little puffs of red dust, lifted by the plunging hoofs of passing teams, dispersed in a grimy shower upon the recumbent man. The sun sank lower and lower; and still Sandy stirred not.[3]

And another of the heroine in her classroom:

Miss Mary had risen, and, in the gathering twilight, had felt her way to the

[2] Ibid., XX.
[3] Bret Harte, *Novels and Stories*, 10 vols., Fireside Edition (Boston and New York, 1910), I, 73. Hereafter this edition will be designated as *Novels and Stories*.

open window. She stood there, leaning against the casement, her eyes fixed on the last rosy tints that were fading from the western sky. There was still some of its light on her pure young forehead, on her white collar, on her clasped white hands, but all fading slowly away.[4]

A limited quantity of sheer ostentation of this sort is tolerable, provided it is not too hopelessly detached from the leading narrative interest.

"Brown of Calaveras" is another example of aesthetic exhibitionism. Although the handsome gambler, Jack Hamlin, making his debut in this story is so cultivated in appearance as to suggest little kinship with the rough country through which he rides, Harte delays the narrative process for two pages to build a series of theatrical pictures. The author appears to admire his own handiwork:

Mr. Hamlin...looked out on the town of Wingdam, now sleeping peacefully, – its harsh outline softened and subdued, its glaring colors mellowed and sobered in the moonlight that flowed over all.... Then he looked up at the firmament, and as he did so a star shot across the twinkling field. Presently another and then another.[5]

"How Old Man Plunkett Went Home" is blameworthy in a slightly different way. It contains all the materials for a good story, but the setting is not properly assimilated. This is typical:

It was dusty in Monte Flat. The ruins of the long dry season were crumbling everywhere: everywhere the drying summer had strewn its red ashes a foot deep, or exhaled its last breath in a red cloud above the troubled highways. The alders and cotton-woods that marked the line of water-courses, were grimy with dust, and looked as if they might have taken root in the open air. The gleaming stones of the parched water-courses themselves were as dry bones in the valley of death. The dusty sunset at times painted the flanks of the distant hills a dull, copper hue: on other days, there was an odd, indefinable earthquake halo on the volcanic cones of the farther coast-spurs. Again an acrid, resinous smoke from the burning wood on Heavytree Hill smarted the eyes, and choked the free breath of Monte Flat; or a fierce wind, driving everything, including the shrivelled summer, like a curled leaf before it, swept down the flanks of the Sierras, and chased the inhabitants to the doors of their cabins, and shook its red fist in at their windows.[6]

---

[4] Ibid., 86.
[5] Ibid., 103-4.
[6] *Writings*, II, 230.

The natural setting here is rich in colors, loaded with similes and personifications; in fact, all the senses are assaulted with striking images. Close discipline is seriously lacking; integration and compactness have given place to aimless descriptive copy.

In "Mrs. Skagg's Husbands", the title story of the 1873 volume, Harte is apparently still further multiplying his strokes in painting the setting: he seems willing to include all details, as if nothing the eye can see were too insignificant, or as if the task of making a choice were too burdensome. His close observation almost runs amuck, as this scene illustrates:

> Their way lay along the flank of Table Mountain, – a wandering trail through a tangled solitude that might have seemed virgin and unbroken but for a few oyster-cans, yeast powder tins, and empty bottles that had been apparently stranded by the "first low wash" of pioneer waves. On the ragged trunk of an enormous pine hung a few tufts of gray hair caught from a passing grizzley, but in strange juxtaposition at its foot lay an empty bottle of incomparable bitter, – the *chef-d'oeuvre* of a hygienic civilization, and blazoned with the arms of an all-healing republic. The head of a rattlesnake peered from a case that had contained tobacco, which was still brightly placarded with the high-colored effigy of a popular *danseuse*.[7]

Harte's delusion is, apparently, that all data are relevant.

Almost all of Harte's longer stories and novels lapse into merely beautiful or impressive scenery. Some of those not yet mentioned in which setting functions poorly are "A Passage in the Life of Mr. John Oakhurst" (1875),[8] in which a gambler takes an early-morning walk in a flower garden; "Left Out on Lone Star Mountain" (1884),[9] in which portions of moonlight scenery too exquisite for the simple character to appreciate are passed directly to the aesthetic reader; "Salomy Jane's Kiss" (1898),[10] in which "the peaceful vista" is admittedly of little interest to the vigilantes and their victims;[11] "The Boom in the 'Calaveras Clarion'" (1899),[12] in which elaborate "sylvan surroundings" are momentarily dangled before the eyes of a busy young editor and then forgotten;

[7] *Novels and Stories*, II, 14.
[8] *Writings*, II, 171 ff.
[9] Ibid., IV, 192 ff.
[10] Ibid., XV, 238 ff.
[11] Ibid., 242.
[12] Ibid., XVI, 161 ff.

and *Gabriel Conroy*, a rambling novel in which Harte's most elaborate snow scene serves as introduction. Most of Harte's experiments
in adapting the Western scene to fictional form were unsuccessful
because he was seldom willing to submit his enthusiasm for the
subject to the rigid discipline of this literary form.

The question arises, Why did not Harte continue to use the
superior technique he exhibited in the *Luck* volume? In the first
place, Harte probably felt no need to integrate after his reputation
assured a market for any sort of work; in the second place, he
was writing in a new field, as were all local colorists of the period,
and was obliged to experiment without a very adequate conception
of the artistic principles involved; and finally, Harte promptly
separated himself from the source of his material so that he was
forced to write from memory instead of immediate observation.
Harte belonged to that majority of local colorists whose imagina-
tions needed the stimulus of living models; and though memory
does not necessarily produce stereotyped patterns, it tends in that
direction. Though the scenes are never quite so much at fault in
this respect as the characters, there are several types of exteriors
of which he was always especially fond: the snowscene, the sea
coast (rugged or sand), the luxurious green forest, the vast and
rugged mountain range, the large river bordered by the tules, the
mining plant and its village.

Mark Twain, like Bret Harte, often felt a compulsion to ornament his settings, especially when writing about the West. An
apt journalist of the West, Twain alternated in his attitudes toward
its content from extreme realism to exuberant romanticism according to his moods. Yet, when he came to use the Western experience
in his narrative art, his taste and instinct for structural economy usually enabled him to resist the temptation to overindulge in descriptive setting. He boasts facetiously that his *The American
Claimant* is "an attempt to pull a book through without the weather".[13] Weather is natural and necessary, he explains, but it ought
to be put in the appendix "where it will not interrupt the flow of
the narrative".

---

[13] "The Weather in this Book", *The American Claimant* (New York, 1892).

And, quite consistently, there is little setting material of any sort that does not have an important function in Mark Twain's long narratives; in the short stories, with a very few notable exceptions, there is practically no setting material except that used for burlesque. Mark Twain cleverly satirizes the descriptive manner of his contemporaries in the initial scene of "The Esquimau Maiden's Romance".[14] The deliberate false note here is produced by framing a theatrical word picture in which the splashy-colored back drop completely misses the tone suggested by the character and her actions:

She had been absently scraping blubber-grease from her cheeks with a small bone-knife and transferring it to her fur sleeve, while she watched the Aurora Borealis swing its flaming streamers out of the sky and wash the lonely snow-plain and the templed icebergs with the rich hues of the prism, a spectacle of almost intolerable splendor and beauty.[15]

As one continues the story it is only too evident that the scenery is a deliberate fraud. Likewise the gaudy and badly arranged scenery in "A Doubled-Barreled Detective Story" (1902) serves to satirize the absurd use of setting as well as other faults of the melodramatic short fiction of the day:

The first scene is in the country, in Virginia; the time, 1880.[16]

October is the time – 1900; Hope Canon is the place, a silver-mining camp away down in the Esmeralda region. It is a secluded spot, high and remote; recent as to discovery; thought by its occupants to be rich in metal – a year or two's prospecting will decide that matter one way or the other.[17]

It is now almost midnight, and in five minutes the new morning will begin. The scene is in the tavern billiard-room.[18]

The tavern dining-room had been cleared of all its furniture save one six-foot pine table and a chair. This table was against one end of the room; the chair was on it; Sherlock Holmes, stately, imposing, impressive, sat in the chair. The public stood. The room was full. The tobacco smoke was dense, the stillness profound.[19]

14 *Cosmopolitan*, November, 1893. See Merle Johnson, *A Bibliography of Mark Twain*, 12.
15 *Mark Twain's Works*, V, 136.
16 Ibid., 285.
17 Ibid., 305-306.
18 Ibid., 315.
19 Ibid., 337.

Twain's prize piece of burlesque in this tale is his imitation of the sentimental use of intrusive scenery. This paragraph is a famous hoax:

It was a crisp and spicy morning in early October. The lilacs and laburnums, lit with the glory-fires of autumn, hung burning and flashing in the upper air, a fairy bridge provided by kind Nature for the wingless wild things that have their homes in the tree-tops and would visit together; the larch and the pomegranate flung their purple and yellow flames in brilliant broad splashes along the slanting sweep of the woodland; the sensuous fragrance of innumerable deciduous flowers rose upon the swooning atmosphere; far in the empty sky a solitary esophagus slept upon motionless wing; everywhere brooded stillness, serenity, and the peace of God.[20]

According to a later statement[21] by the author, the only comment ever made to him upon this passage was in the form of inquiries concerning the word *esophagus*. One learned professor found the passage "a very touching and beautiful one" except for this troublesome word; another professor, a New Englander, read the story "with much gratification and edification" but also demanded to know "What in hell is an esophagus?" The author was delighted with the success of the trick:

that paragraph was most ably constructed [he confessed] for the deception it was intended to put upon the reader. It was my intention that it should read plausibly, and...that it should be emotional and touching. Alas, if I had but left that one treacherous word out, I should have scored! scored everywhere; and the paragraph would have slidden through every reader's sensibilities like oil, and left not a suspicion behind.[22]

Twain's burlesque of landscape and scenery continues with a ludicrous minuteness of detail, as he wanders on in ridiculous irrelevancy:

On both sides of the canyon the mountains rise wall-like, three thousand feet, and the long spiral of straggling huts down in its narrow bottom gets a kiss from the sun only once a day, when he sails over at noon. The village is a couple of miles long; the cabins stand well apart from each other. The tavern is the only "frame" house – the only house, one might say. It occupies a central position, and is the evening resort of the population. They

20 Ibid., 304.
21 Springfield *Republican*, April 12, 1902. See *Works*, V, 304-306 n.
22 *Works*, V, 305 n.

drink there, and play seven-up and dominoes; also billiards, for there is a table, crossed all over with torn places repaired with court plaster; there are some cues, but no leathers; some chipped balls which clatter when they run, and do not slow up gradually, but stop suddenly and sit down; there is a part of a cube of chalk, with a projecting jag of flint in it; and the man who can score six on a single break can set up the drinks at the bar's expense.[23]

Another prolonged hoax, "The Enemy Conquered, or Love Triumphant" (1893), purports to be taken from an old manuscript by one G. Ragsdale McClintock and given to Twain by Mr. Cable. The theatrical background is a burlesque aimed not only at Cable, but apparently at Harte, Mary Noailles Murfree, and others as well. When the hero kisses his lover in a particularly secluded and florescent spot, the author admits that "the scene was overwhelming".[24] There is more than one take-off on the ornamental but unsuccessful use of scenery, such as the following:

Here he stood alone, gazing at the stars; confounded as he was, here he stood. The rippling stream rolled on at his feet. Twilight had already begun to draw her sable mantle over the earth, and now and then the fiery smoke would ascend from the little town which lay spread out before him. The citizens seemed to be full of life and good-humor; but poor Elfanzo saw not a brilliant scene.[25]

The irrelevancy of a brilliant scene which "poor Elfanzo saw not" should have made many a local colorist of the period blush shamefully, Harte especially. In "A Cure for the Blues" (1893), Twain's review of "The Enemy Conquered", we are told that McClintock "does not make the mistake of being relevant on one page and irrelevant on another; he is irrelevant on all of them".[26] In this story, Twain explains, nothing can be omitted; "every sentence that this master has produced may be likened to a perfect set of teeth, white, uniform, beautiful. If you pull one, the charm is gone".[27] The great McClintock was one who

loved to stand up before a dazed world, and pour forth flame and smoke and

[23] Ibid., 307-308.
[24] Ibid., X, 146.
[25] Ibid., 143.
[26] Ibid., 104.
[27] Ibid., 115.

lava and pumice-stone into the skies, and work his subterranean thunders, and shake himself with earthquakes, and stench himself with sulphur fumes;[28]

he leads the reader

from wonder to wonder, through gardens of hidden treasure, where giant streams bloom before you, and behind you, and all around, and you feel as happy, and groggy, and satisfied with your quart of mixed metaphors aboard as you would if it had been mixed in a sample-room and delivered from a jig.[29]

Cable, a very serious writer, stands in sharp contrast to Twain. His descriptions are often so engrossing that the reader submits to the narrative pause which they require. Cable's pictures have emotional value of refined quality; behind every scene lurks a mystery which maintains a particular mood in the reader's mind throughout the story. The illusion of antiquity and depth is effected sometimes through outmoded architecture, carriages, and clothing; sometimes through the unity of man with nature.

"'Sieur George" (1873), the first of the *Scribner's* stories to be published, has a strong local flavor and a descriptive texture that almost overshadows the narrative interest. The suspense in the story is sustained by a single trick, the mystery of the hair trunk; otherwise the background would always dominate. Though the author slightly personifies the chief scene, the "venerable" apartment house where most of the events take place, the setting as a whole is independent of action. Near the end of the story, after 'Sieur George and his foster daughter have parted, the girl accidentally catches a glimpse of the old gentleman. Note the metropolitan description that is used to adorn this momentary event:

Far away southward and westward the river glistened in the sunset. Along its sweeping bends the chimneys of a smoking commerce, the magazines of surplus wealth, the gardens of the opulent, the steeples of a hundred sanctuaries, and thousands on thousands of mansions and hovels covered the fertile birthright arpents which 'Sieur George, in his fifty years' stay, had seen tricked away from dull colonial Esaus by their blue-eyed breth-

[28] Ibid., 101.
[29] Ibid., 108.

ren of the North. Nearer by she looked upon the forlornly silent region of lowly dwellings, neglected by legislation and shunned by all lovers of comfort, that once had been the smiling fields of her own grandsire's broad plantation; and but a little way off, trudging across the marshy commons, her eye caught sight of 'Sieur George following the sunset out upon the prairies to find a night's rest in the high grass.[30]

A significant bit of action is here highlighted by an especially brilliant frame. This device is also used as Old Kookoo, who for fifty years has suppressed a desire to know what is in a mysterious trunk, makes his way to 'Sieur George's apartment:

The November night, as it often does in that region, had grown warm and clear; the stars were sparkling like diamonds pendant in deep blue heavens, and at every window and lattice and cranny the broad, bright moon poured down its glittering beams upon the hoary-headed thief, as he crept along the mouldering galleries and down the ancient corridor.[31]

This picture delays the action but restores the loss in the form of greater dramatic intensity.

The next story, "Tite Poulette" (1874), closely resembles "'Sieur George" in the background it employs. Again the action takes place within and around an interesting building

which still stands, flush with the street, a century old. Its big, round-arched windows in a long second-story row, are walled up, and two or three from time to time have had smaller windows let into them again, with odd little latticed peep-holes in the batten shutters.[32]

The house is of no importance – any house would do; but this house captures the reader's curiosity, both by its mysteriousness and its historical interest. To continue with the story:

All the features of the building lead me to guess that it is a remnant of the old Spanish Barracks, whose extensive structure fell by government sale into private hands a long time ago. At the end toward the swamp a great, oriental-looking passage is left, with an arched entrance, and a pair of ponderous wooden doors. You look at it, and almost see Count O'Reilly's artillery come bumping and trundling out, and dash around into the ancient Plaza to bang away at King St. Charles's birthday.

---

[30] *Old Creole Days* (New York, 1892), 266-67.
[31] Ibid., 265.
[32] Ibid., 213.

Gradually "'Tite Poulette" is dominated by its mixed blood theme and abandons its initial preoccupation with the physical surroundings. But occasionally a character moves into a zone that the author is impelled to describe. In this story, for instance, occurs Cable's first picture of the quadroon ballroom, the *Salle de Conde*. While looking for Zalli, Kopping enters a large hall filled with

a blaze of lamps, a bewildering flutter of fans and floating robes, strains of music, columns of gay promenaders, a long row of turbaned mothers lining either wall, gentlemen of the portlier sort filling the recesses of the windows, whirling waltzers gliding here and there – smiles and grace, smiles and grace; all fair, orderly, elegant, bewitching.[33]

"Madame Delicieuse" (1875) deals with a more cultivated stratum of urban society with more subdued exotic beauty, decayed surroundings, and mystery. The General is recognized as "antiquated", but without narrow seclusion in life, speech, or eccentricities that would class him with 'Sieur George. Like the two preceding stories, "Madame Delicieuse" begins by introducing the houses within which the chief events of the narrative are to be laid – the home of Dr. Mossy, "just adjoining the old Cafe de Poesie on the corner", a "little one-story, yellow-washed tenement ...with its two glass doors protected by batten shutters, and its low, weed-grown tile roof sloping out over the sidewalk";[34] and the house of Madame Delicieuse, a "narrow, red-brick-front mansion", "one of the sights of the Rue Royale", "by night its tall, narrow outline reaching high up toward the stars, with its windows aglow".[35] Cable's introductory descriptions follow a formula.

"The Cafe des Exiles" (1876) opens with a view of the Rue Burgundy, in the year 1835. The scene, said by the narrator to have been constructed from memory after forty years, is vivid and rich with similes:

An antiquated story-and-a-half Creole cottage sitting right down on the banquette, as do the Choctaw squaws who sell hay and sassafras and life-everlasting, with a high close board-fence shutting out of view the diminutive garden on the southern side. An ancient willow droops over the roof

[33] Ibid., 235.
[34] Ibid., 271.
[35] Ibid., 272-73.

of round tiles, and partly hides the discolored stucco, which keeps dropping off into the garden as though the cafe was stripping for the plunge into oblivion – disrobing for its execution. I see, well up in the angle of the broad side gable, shaded by its rude awning of clapboards, as the eyes of an old dame are shaded by her wrinkled hand, the window of Pauline.... I see the top of the fig-tree, the pale green clump of bananas, the tall palmetto with its jagged crown, Pauline's own two orange trees holding up their hands toward the window, heavy with the promises of autumn; the broad crimson mass of many-stemmed oleander, and the crisp bows of the pomegranate loaded with freckled apples, and with here and there a lingering scarlet blossom.[36]

For nine pages the descriptive muse holds full sway, while the atmosphere texture is deliberately woven. The characters, with their habits and customs, are treated separately and collectively, through pictorial, illustrative exposition. Then during the next twenty-four pages there is a minimum of descriptive matter; the story is largely dialogue, and only the new places and persons are described. The illusion of antiquity, strangeness, and mystery is thenceforth maintained by dialects, by unheard-of patterns of conduct, and by the concealment of the real motives of the characters.

"Posson Jone'" (1876) varies from the usual pattern in that the central character appears just before the opening scene. Jules St.-Ange idles on a Sunday morning at the place "where the intersection of Royal and Conti Streets some seventy years ago formed a central corner of New Orleans".[37] There is no clue as to whether or not Jules is affected by the scene – most likely not; but Cable assumes that it will interest the reader:

There had been a hurricane in the night. The weed-brown tile-roofs were still dripping, and from lofty brick and low adobe walls a rising steam responded to the summer sunlight. Up-street, and across the Rue du Canal, one could get glimpses of the gardens in Faubourg Ste. Marie standing in silent wretchedness, so many tearful Lucretias, tattered victims of the storm. Short remnants of the wind now and then came down the narrow street in erratic puffs heavily laden with odors of broken boughs and torn flowers, skimmed the little pools of rain-water in the deep ruts of the unpaved street, and suddenly went away to nothing, like a juggler's butterflies or a young man's money.

[36] Ibid., 85-86.
[37] Ibid., 149.

It was very picturesque, the Rue Royal. The rich and poor met together. The locksmith's swinging key creaked next door to the bank; across the way, crouching, mendicant-like, in the shadow of a great importing house, was the mud laboratory of the mender of broken combs. Light balconies overhung the rows of showy shops and stores open for trade this Sunday morning, and pretty Latin faces of the higher class glanced over their savagely-pronged railings upon the passers below. At some windows hung lace curtains, flannel duds at some, and at others only the scraping and sighing one-hinged shutter groaning toward Paris after its neglectful master.[38]

The initial background laid, the narrative begins, and only when the action repairs to a particularly picturesque new quarter does the descriptive muse become pronounced. For example:

The street they now entered was a quiet one. The eye of any chance passer would have been at once drawn to a broad, heavy, white brick edifice on the lower side of the way, with a flagpole standing out like a bowsprit from one of its great windows, and a pair of lamps hanging before a large closed entrance. It was a theatre, honey-combed with gambling-dens. At this morning hour all was still, and the only sign of life was a knot of little barefoot girls gathered within its narrow shade, and each carrying an infant relative.[39]

"Madame Delphine" (1881), a novelette of short story texture, devotes its first chapter, entitled "An Old House", almost entirely to an atmospheric description of the primary scene of the story. The first portion of this chapter so well illustrates Cable's formula that it will bear quotation:

A few steps from the St. Charles Hotel, in New Orleans, brings you to and across Canal Street, the central avenue of the city, and to that corner where the flower-women sit at the inner and outer edges of the arcaded sidewalk, and make the air sweet with fragrant merchandise. The crowd – and if it is near the time of the carnival it will be great – will follow Canal Street.

But you turn, instead, into the quiet, narrow way which a lover of Creole antiquity, in fondness for a romantic past, is still prone to call the Rue Royal. You will pass a few restaurants, a few auction-rooms, a few furniture warehouses, and will hardly realize that you have left behind you the activity and clatter of a city of merchants before you find yourself in a region of architectural decrepitude, where an ancient and foreign-seeming

---

[38] Ibid., 150-51.
[39] Ibid., 160.

domestic life, in second stories, overhangs the ruins of a former commercial prosperity, and upon everything has settled down a long sabbath of decay. The vehicles in the street are few in number, and are merely passing through; the stores are shrunken into shops; you see here and there, like a patch of bright mould, the stall of that significant fungus, the Chinaman. Many great doors are shut and clamped and grown gray with cobweb; many street windows are nailed up; half the balconies are begrimed and rust-eaten, and many of the humid arches and alleys which characterize the older Franco-Spanish piles of stuccoed brick betray a squalor almost oriental.

Yet beauty lingers here. To say nothing of the picturesque, sometimes you get sight of comfort, sometimes of opulence, through the unlatched wicket in some *porte-cochere*-red-painted brick pavement, foliage of dark palm of pale banana, marble or granite masonry and blossomy parterres; or through a chink between some pair of heavy batten window-shutters, opened with an almost reptile weariness, your eye gets a glimpse of lace and brocade upholstery, silver and bronze, and much similar rich antiquity.[40]

This general picture is more suggestive of a tourist's guide to the city of New Orleans than a short story. Aside from fixing an atmosphere, it stands as a detached prelude. At last the author describes the particular house in which the characters live as

a small, low, brick house of a story and a half, set out upon the sidewalk, as weather-beaten and mute as an aged beggar fallen asleep. Its corrugated roof of full red tiles, sloping down toward you with an inward curve, is overgrown with weeds, and in the fall of the year is gay with the yellow plumes of the goldenrod. You can almost touch with your cane the low edge of the broad, over-hanging eaves. The batten shutters at door and window, with hinges like those of a postern, are shut with a grip that makes one's knuckles and nails feel lacerated. Save in the brick-work itself there is not a cranny. You would say the house has the lockjaw. There are two doors, and to each a single chipped and battered marble step. Continuing on down the sidewalk, on a line with the house, is a garden masked from view by a high, close board-fence. You may see the tops of its fruit-trees – pomegranate, peach, banana, fig, pear, and particularly one large orange, close by the fence, that must be very old.[41]

Within the story proper, background ornamentation is reserved for a new scene or for a dramatic or lyrical pause. Such a pause comes, for example, as the hero is about to meet his lover. The narrator's eloquence presages an intense experience:

[40] Ibid., 1-2.
[41] Ibid., 3.

It was one of those Southern nights under whose spell all the sterner energies of the mind cloak themselves and lie down in bivouac, and the fancy and the imagination, that cannot sleep, slip their fetters and escape, beckoned away from behind every flowering bush and sweet-smelling tree, and every stretch of lonely, half-lighted walk, by the genius of poetry. The air stirred softly now and then, and was still again, as if the breezes lifted their expectant pinions and lowered them once more, awaiting the rising of the moon in a silence which fell upon the fields, the roads, the gardens, the walls, and the suburban and half-suburban streets, like a pause in worship.[42]

Then Vignevielle enters a

many-flowered garden, among whose untrimmed rose trees and tangled vines, and often, also, in its old walks of flowered shell, the coco-grass and crabgrass had spread riotously, and sturdy weeds stood up in bloom.[43]

and there, eventually, "an outline – a presence – a form – a spirit – a girl!" is discovered.

A companion story to "Posson Jone'", though widely removed in chronology, is "Pere Raphael" (1901). It is fitted into precisely the same setting. Although "Posson Jone'" "had a hard time getting into print",[44] Cable explained, it nevertheless fulfilled his own requirements for a story; in fact, it "so satisfied by easily pleased fancy and found its way so steadily, though slowly, into the favor of the readers" that it finally occurred to him "that another story of the same time, place, and circumstance might be lying beneath it, like one painting beneath another in the same frame and on the same canvas".[45] Consequently, he resolved to revisit the region, "to go with seeking eyes". He "had not left the sight five steps behind" when he found all the material he needed.

I might admit that for striking effect the moment was fortunate [he states], were it not that in that region I have never known when it was not fortunate. At any rate, the court's green-brown flagging was shining wet, and repeated all those good lines and daring colors in its mirror.[46]

Thus, notebook in hand, Cable noted the facts, and "by the

[42] Ibid., 41.
[43] Ibid., 42.
[44] "*Posson Jone'*" *and Pere Raphael* (New York, 1909), 15.
[45] Ibid., 12-13.
[46] Ibid., 8-9.

spot's warrant of antiquity, romance, and picturesque decay", added "Pere Raphael" to the earlier story, the two appearing in a beautifully illustrated edition, *"Posson Jone'" and Pere Raphael* (1909). "Pere Raphael" is a rather ingenious piece of literary manipulation; but confined to the shadows of the earlier story, it would have failed through the artificiality of its pattern, not to mention other weaknesses. The atmosphere that enshrouds the earlier tale and lends it credibility is dissipated in "Pere Raphael". This story is, in the first place, too much taken up with new half-depicted characters and sheer plot machinery to attend to background, and in the second place it reveals a loss of descriptive power. Even the best pictures in the newer work are hollow echoes of his earlier success. Observe the matter-of-factness, the absence of fresh and powerful figures, the lack of discriminate detail in these scenes:

The St. Ange house stood on the Swamp side of the Rue Royale, next to a corner of that very intersection with Conti Street where Jones and Jules first met. It opened on the sidewalk and had at its ground floor, extending from the street-door steps on its right to the porte-cochere on the left, a narrow, hooded balcony masked by a lattice along its sidewalk face and across its porte-cochere end. In the great batten gate of the porte-cochere was the usual small one for servants, in the balcony lattice, a very small hinged window. Into this balcony let also the long French windows of the drawing-room. Its unlatticed end, by the front door, was fair with potted flowers, and through the railing there one might pass to the steps and the street.[47]

Madame Merrifield's tall house, in which, this afternoon, she was taking some of the sleep owing to her from the night, stood flush with the sidewalk, with its garden on one side, at the corner of the two streets. Through its oleanders and myrtles and its high wooden fence of graceful open-work one got a broken view of the rude Place Congo, in a part of which a great multitude were gathered on the broad seats of Cayetano's amphitheatre to see his buffalo-and-tiger fight.[48]

There is little emotional power to be found in such description. Cable's notebook habit has led him into achitectural blue-printing; good artistic description demands powerfully suggestive details, not exhaustive facts. In a reference to "Pere Raphael",

[47] Ibid., 75-76.
[48] Ibid., 130-31.

Cable exclaimed: "Oh, mark you; this is no builded fiction, but the clean sand of fact as I noted it down right there lest I *might* let imagination impose on memory."[49] In this story Cable shows himself a more conventional local colorist than on other occasions. Unfortunately his most accurate descriptions are seldom his best. The atmosphere in which he specialized required vagueness, an incompleteness of fact to be supplied from the reader's imagination. This is lacking in "Pere Raphael".

In the early eighties, while Cable's Louisiana stories were almost a regular feature in *Scribner's*, Mary Noailles Murfree of Tennessee began her spectacular but brief literary triumph in the *Atlantic* with fiction fresh from the Cumberland Mountains. Though her narrative art was not perfect enough in all particulars to win her a permanent reputation, she is of special importance in this study for having shown more ingenuity than any of her contemporaries in her experiments with short-story settings.

Tennessee scenery is so extensively portrayed in all of her work that it is usually possible to account for the success or failure of each of her stories by studying the relation which its setting bears to its structure as a whole. Murfree's limited first-hand knowledge of the secluded life which she chose to interpret, and the absence of complex intellectual and social traditions in this remote region, prevented her from achieving an atmosphere as distinctive and compelling as that of Cable. Though a purely emotional integration like Cable's was not within her capacity, she integrated her best stories structurally, giving her settings a function of sufficient importance to justify their length and emphasis. And in her experimental efforts toward this end, she was able to develop special setting techniques which her predecessors had only suggested.

Almost all of Murfree's stories contain descriptive passages eloquent in diction and correspondingly insignificant in function. Yet this defect is sometimes not evident for the reason that in some stories the descriptive material has a vital function in the story. Most of Murfree's stories with only a simple use of setting are failures, for she could generally use setting successfully only by

---

[49] Ibid., 10.

integrating it with character or personifying it to function as character.

In Murfree's earliest mountain stories, written before her descriptive method was fully mature, a purely ornamental use of background is characteristic. This is true of her first mountain story, "Taking the Blue Ribbon at the County Fair" (*Atlantic*, 1878). Here the writer shows a flair for colorful background, a sense of the picturesque, an undue intensity, and an obvious artificiality. After Cynthia Hollis' anticipation of her lover's proposal had brought her a rebuke, she

stood watching him until the laurel bushes hid him from sight; then sliding from the door-frame to the step, she sat motionless, a bright-hued mass of yellow-draperies and red peppers, her slumberous deep eyes resting on the leaves that have closed upon him.

She was the central figure of a still landscape. The mid-day sunshine fell in broad effulgence upon it; the homely, dun-colored shadows had been running away all morning, as if shirking the contrast with the splendors of the golden light, until nothing was left of them except a dark circle beneath the widespreading trees.[50]

"The Dancin' Party at Harrison's Cove" (also *Atlantic*, 1878), though a vastly superior story from the standpoint of characterization, is also weakened by its purely descriptive backgrounds. In no way is the story carried forward by such occasional pictures as the following:

An early moon was riding, clear and full, over this wild spur of the Alleghenies; the stars are few and very faint; even the great Scorpio lurked, vaguely outlined, above the wooded ranges; and the white mist, that filled the long, deep, narrow valley between the parallel lines of the mountains, shimmered with opalescent gleams.[51]

To see what happened to this type of setting in the later stories, we may examine "The Bushwhacker", titular story in the collection of 1899. Primarily a character story, it opens with Hilary Knox's climb to a rocky promontory. While the young mountaineer stands "breathless with eager expectation", the author takes seven pages to paint a landscape which the character completely ignores. There

50 *The Mystery of Witch-Face Mountain* (Boston and New York, 1896), 176.
51 *In the Tennessee Mountains* (Boston and New York, 1887), 215.

is apparently no effort at concordance between the character and his surroundings. Soon the author shifts from the immediate situation to the habitual, and we learn incidentally that Hilary's appearances here have occasioned some concern on the part of the birds that inhabit the peaks. So willing is the author to digress that the mere mention of birds leads to a two-page discourse on that subject. We finally leave the passage without any hint of a connection between birds and Hilary Knox. Euphuism and ostentation are widely evident; for instance, the author uses this elaborate landscape figure to turn the page on the calendar:

And when, as in sudden enchantment, darkness became light and night developed into dawn, when color renewed the landscape, and the dull sky grew red as if flushed with sudden triumph, and the black mountains turned royally purple in the distance and tenderly green nearer at hand, and the waters of the rivers leaped and flashed like a live thing, as with an actual joy in existence, and the fiery sun, full of vital yellow flame, flared up over the eastern horizon, the squadron... rode forth into a new day.[52]

Such passages reveal the puerility of fluency without emotion. But this is hardly as objectionable as setting which actually clashes with the mood of a character. With suspense at a low ebb, the reader may be scarcely aware of intrusive matter; but when a crippled youth hotly pursued by armed soldiers is dashing for cover, neither he nor the reader will be satisfied to wait long enough to observe that

the rude, unplastered, whitewashed walls were illuminated by moonlight, for all down one side of the long apartment the windows overlooking the gorge were full of white radiance, and in glittering squares it lay upon the floor.[53]

The reflective calm suggested by such description has little place in a zone of desperate action.

Neither in the earlier stories nor the later was Murfree able to reach a high artistic level while using setting independently in the story. In the early stories the settings are flat and unimpressive; in the later ones all sense of proportion and fitness is lost.

Like Murfree, Thomas Nelson Page seems to have felt a patri-

[52] *The Bushwhackers and Other Stories* (Chicago and New York, 1899), 33-34.
[53] Ibid., 104.

otic desire to save the rich material around him. More specifically, he was motivated, says Mims, partly by an artistic impulse and partly by the "ideal of preserving in some sort a picture of a civilization which, once having sweetened the life of the South, has since then well nigh perished from the earth".[54] So lovingly does Page treat this material in his fiction that critics almost universally agree that his pictures are immoderately idealized; yet Page seems at least to have aimed at an unprejudiced point of view.

But Page's experimentation with techniques is not highly original. There is one way, however, in which he went beyond his precedents: he exploited, more than any other local colorist, the full historical value of a scene. In description he was able to draw forth images already in the reader's dim memory. Though Page's settings are brief and generally employed only as background and ornament, they exhibit a rigid economy and a high literary efficiency. Almost unique in this respect among the Southern local colorists, Page never allowed his enthusiasm for the picturesqueness of his region to spoil his literary proportion.

About fifty of Page's sixty short stories have settings used only for background and ornament. In the stories set on a typical plantation the details are few and brief – the background is only roughly blocked in. But in the handful of stories depicting some unknown part of the country, the descriptions are lengthened and the setting given a more significant role. Whenever a story is set in a remote rural locality, Page sometimes ornaments as pictorially as a conventional local colorist. For example, in "Little Darby" (1894):

The sun was just rising above the pines, filling the little bottom between the cabins with a sort of rosy light, and making the dewy bushes and weeds sparkle with jewel-strung gossamer webs, when Little Darby, with his musket in his hand, stepped for the last time out of the low door.[55]

The typical Page landscapes, however, are seldom decorative. The Virginia plantations upon which his greatest stories are laid are all drawn according to a brief, conservative pattern. Yet there

[54] Edwin Mims, "Thomas Nelson Page", *Atlantic Monthly*, C, 110 (July, 1907), 107.
[55] *The Burial of the Guns* (New York, 1900), 202.

is little repetition in phrase or image because each is built up with a slightly different set of details. In "Marse Chan" (1884), the author's first and greatest plantation story, the general background is thus presented:

> Their once splendid mansions, now fast falling to decay, appeared to view from time to time, set back far from the road, in proud seclusion, among groves of oak and hickory, now scarlet and gold with the early frost.[56]

Particularly the traveller notices "the handsome old place half a mile off from the road":

> The numerous out-buildings and the large barns and stables told that it had once been the seat of wealth, and the wild waste of sassafras that covered the broad fields gave it an air of desolation that greatly excited my interest.[57]

With no more descriptive detail, the story connected with the place is related in dialect by the old Negro standing by the fence. Rarely is there a glimpse of the background behind the action of the characters, and then we find only the most common objects mentioned:

> 'Twuz always ridin' or fishin' down dyah in de river; or sometime he' go over dyah, an' 'im an' she'd go an' set in de yard onder de trees; she wuz knittin' some sort o' bright-cullored some'n,' wid de grass growin' all up 'g'inst her.[58]

> De moon come out, an' I catch sight o' her stan'in' dyar in her white dress, wid de cloak she had wrapped herse'f up in drapped off on de groun'. ...She wuz mons'us purty ez she stood dyar wid de green bushes behine her.[59]

In "Unc' Edinburg's Drowndin'" (1886), another tale related by an old Negro servant, the glances at the landscape are even briefer. At the beginning of this story we are told that "the time was Christmas Eve, and the place the muddiest road in eastern Virginia".[60] Once during the narrative we see two young lovers on the plantation lawn for an instant, where "dee walk so slow

---

[56] *In Ole Virginia* (New York, 1922), 1.
[57] Ibid., 2.
[58] Ibid., 10-11.
[59] Ibid., 26.
[60] Ibid., 39.

down dem walks in de shade you got to sight 'em by a tree to tell ef de movin' 'tall."[61]

"Meh Lady: A Story of the War" (1886) follows the same pattern. There is no picture of the plantation as a whole, but the reader's imaginative conception of it is supported by occasional glimpses at certain parts of it, particularly the vegetation. The initial scene opens with the typical narrator, old and black, "standing in the dogwood bushes just below me... where the little footpath through the straggling pines and underbush ran over it". Uncle Billy recalls that Meh Lady followed her brother "down to de mill-pond th'oo briers an' ev'ywhar",[62] and Captain Wilton walked "to dat red rose-bush an' pull two or th'ee roses".[63] He remembers his own sweet reminiscence:

I wuz settin' in de do' wid mah pipe,...an' de moon sort o' meltin' over de yard, an' I sort o' got to studyin', an' hit 'pear like de plantation 'live once mo', an' de ain' no mo' scufflin', an' de ole times done come back ag'in, an' I heah meh Kerridge-horses stompin' in de stalls, an' de place all cleared up ag'in, an' fence all roun' de pahsture, an' I smell de wet clover-blossoms right good.[64]

"Polly" (1886) is a continuation of the preceding stories as far as setting is concerned. With Bob, Polly "used to run wild over the place,... climbing cherry-trees, and fishing in the creek";[65] later "she was strolling through the old flower-garden with a tall young fellow...who was so careful as to hold aside the long branches of the rose-bushes".[66] The weather was generally appropriate: "the summer had gone, and the Indian summer had come in its place, hazy, dreamy, and sad".[67]

The county estate of the Major in "George Washington's Last Duel" (1890) is apparently assumed to be like all the other Page plantations, but in "My Cousin Fanny" (1894) the residential setting shows some note of distinction without violating the pattern.

[61] Ibid., 57.
[62] Ibid., 89.
[63] Ibid., 106.
[64] Ibid., 138.
[65] Ibid., 190-91.
[66] Ibid., 202.
[67] Ibid., 210.

Woodside, the ancient family domain, is pictured more specifically than its prototypes in the earlier stories, but it differs only in being a bit older and more pretentious than usual:

The house was a large brick edifice, with a pyramidal roof, covered with moss, small windows, porticos with pillars somewhat out of repair, a big high hall, and a staircase wide enough to drive a gig up it if it could have turned the corners. A grove of great forest oaks and poplars densely shaded it, and made it look rather gloomy; and the garden, with the old graveyard covered with periwinkle at one end was almost in front while the other side of the wood – a primeval forest, from which the place took its name – came up so close as to form a strong, dark background.[68]

After the war the old place presented a notable contrast:

The fields were poor, and grew up in briars and sassafras, and the house was too large and out of repair to keep from decay.[69]

Other later stories which make use of the typical plantation setting are "The Long Hillside" (1904), "Old Jabe's Marital Experiments" (1904), "Mam' Lyddy's Recognition" (1904), and especially "The Christmas Peace" (1904).

One other background pattern is characteristic of Page's stories, the battle fields of the war. A bit of the actual fighting is found in "Marse Chan" and "Meh Lady", but "The Burial of the Guns" (1894) is the earliest story to make much use of descriptive detail. In this story the battlefield is obscured by an atmosphere in which an impression of antiquity is reinforced by an element of pathos:

Thus the old battery, on an April evening of 1865, found itself toiling alone up the steep mountain road which leads above the river to the gap, which formed the chief pass in that part of the Blue Ridge. Both men and horses looked, in the dim and waning light of the gray April day, rather like shadows of the beings themselves. And anyone seeing them toiling painfully up, the thin horses floundering in the mud, and the men, often up to their knees, tugging at the sinking wheels,...might have thought them the ghosts of some old battery lost from some long and forgotten war on that deep and desolate mountain road.[70]

---

[68] *The Burial of the Guns,* 4.
[69] Ibid., 2.
[70] Ibid., 58.

The Colonel has been ordered to hold that pass at all costs, and to that end he selects a location for his battery.

The last streak of twilight brought them to the top of the pass; his soldier's instinct and a brief recognizance made earlier in the day told him that this was his place, and before daybreak next morning the point was as well fortified as a night's work by weary and supperless men could make it. A prettier spot could not have been found for the purpose; a small plateau, something over an acre in extent, where a charcoal-burner's hut had once stood, lay right at the top of the pass. It was a little higher on either side than in the middle, where a small brook, along which the charcoal-burner's track was yet visible, came down from the wooded mountain above, thus giving a natural crest to aid the fortifications on either side, with open space for the guns, while the edge of the wood coming down from the mountain afforded shelter for the camp.[71]

The most intimate pictures of the war are found in "Little Darby" (1894), a story which traces with descriptive detail the part played by a backwoods Southerner. A few of the most exciting encounters occur before such backgrounds as the following:

The only break in the ditches was a gate opening into the field right on top of the hill. The gate was gone, but two huge wooden gate-posts, each a tree-trunk, still stood and barred the way. No cannon had room to turn in between them; a battery had tried and a pile of dead men, horses, and debris marked its failure.[72]

The company after a fierce charge found itself hugging the ground in a wide field, on the far side of which the enemy – infantry and artillery – was posted in force. Lying down they were pretty well protected from the artillery; and lying down, the infantry generally, even with their better guns, could not hurt them to a great extent; but a line of sharp-shooters, well placed behind cover of scattered rocks on the far side of the field, could reach them with their long-range rifles.[73]

The slope down and the slope up to the group of rocks behind which he lay were both in plain view, and any man would be riddled who attempted to cross the rock; and though the ground in that direction dipped a little, there was one little ridge in full view of both lines and perfectly bare, except for a number of bodies of skirmishers who had fallen earlier in the day.[74]

[71] Ibid., 59.
[72] Ibid., 213-14.
[73] Ibid., 220-21.
[74] Ibid., 222.

It was a scene of utter desolation that he passed through, for the country was the seat of war; fences were gone, woods burnt, and the fields cut up and bare; and it rained all the time.[75]

James Lane Allen, an ardent student of narrative art and a competent local color theorist, took his setting art quite seriously and used it with a variety of functions. His talent for simple scenic description was evident in many of his stories, including "Too Much Momentum" (*Harper's*, 1885). Here the rural background is, like that of his poetry, sweet and idyllic. Professor Evers' farm house "lay with something like ideal beauty in the foreground of his pastoral landscape".[76] The background, the farm itself,

was a paradise of bloom and music, of greenness and running waters. These were woodlands crowned heavily by huge walnuts of immemorial youth; maples so green when all the woods are brown; king oaks from whose topmost bough the squirrel dropped with painless fall; benign elms on whose far-reaching arms the vine slept the summer through, or, waking, reached outward to embrace the ash, which pale and tender, loves to grow apart; and mighty avenues of water-seeking sycamores with leopard-spotted limbs.[77]

The scene proves to be only a backdrop, despite the poetic figures tending to bring it to life. It is not at all essential to the plot or characters of the story, but has a certain poetic or atmospheric value that is effective enough in an independent way.

Allen's next stories, those in the *Flute and Violin* volume, are, in Pattee's opinion, defective with respect to setting; "they make often too much use of the natural background". In Allen's first period, Pattee continues, his

canvas was small, his plots single and uncomplicated, his backgrounds over-elaborate, impeding the movement of the plot and overshadowing the characters.[78]

This judgment is a rather broad statement in view of the fact that it could not apply to more than half of the collection. "Flute and Violin" (*Harper's*, 1890) contains no landscaping whatsoever

[75] Ibid., 228.
[76] *Harper's New Monthly Magazine*, LXX, 702(April, 1885).
[77] Ibid., 701.
[78] Pattee, *American Literature Since 1870*, 367.

and could scarcely be called a local story. Even more universal is "Posthumous Fame" (*Century*, 1890), a purely ethical story in a half-rhetorical tone. "King Solomon of Kentucky" (*Century*, 1889), as the title suggests, is set in a definite place, but the setting could hardly be said to dominate. The movement is so slow in this story that the scenes, mostly old buildings and streets of Lexington, the "Athens of the West", described in a Cable-like manner, can scarcely be said to interrupt any dramatic action. There is apparently more interest in authenticity than in spectacle. The author assures the reader, in fact, that "scarce the name of a character or a line of description in this tale but was taken from the local history of the time".[79] There is considerable atmospheric value in the pictures of the city during different stages of the plague. For example:

Grass grew in the deserted streets. Gardens became little wildernesses of rank weeds and riotous creepers. Around shut window-lattices roses clambered and shed their perfume into the poisoned air, or dropped their faded petals to strew the echoless thresholds. In darkened rooms family portraits gazed on sad vacancy or looked helplessly down on rigid sheeted forms.

In the trees of poplar and locust along the streets the unmolested birds built and brooded. The oriole swung its hempen nest from a bough covering the door of the spider-tenanted factory, and in front of the old Medical Hall the blue-jay shot up his angry crest and screamed harshly down at the passing bier.[80]

But a close examination of the *Flute and Violin* collection shows Pattee's general charge of over-elaborateness to be entirely unjust; in fact, Allen, in relation to other local colorists of his period, is unusually conservative in his descriptive settings in this early volume. A few of his latest stories, such as "Ash Can" (*Century*, 1921), "Miss Locke" (*Century*, 1922), and *The Alabaster Box* (New York, 1923), are so much of an ethical and universal cast that they include, like "Posthumous Fame", almost no setting at all. And the tales and novels which belong to Allen's productive middle years reveal a use of setting that, considered as a whole, rises above the level of mere background and ornament.

[79] "Introductory Sketch", *Flute and Violin and Other Kentucky Tales and Romances* (New York, 1908), x.
[80] Ibid., 89.

It is sometimes asserted that Sarah Orne Jewett, the most "local" as well as "vocal" of the New Englanders, never was a fashionable local colorist in the sense of using, on occasions, purely decorative setting material. No one of her group had a greater fondness for color. Chapman's claim that she was "beautifully free" from "all this description-at-a-distance" – that "she never bores us with mere description for description's sake"[81] – is hardly tenable. Lowell wrote of her, in his old age: "She is lenient in landscape, a great merit, I think, in these days".[82] Pattee claims that "she refused to yield to the demands of the time" – that "she wrote to please herself, to satisfy her own artistic requirements".[83] Though she did not consider colorful descriptions as essential to literary merit, she was obviously guilty of such descriptions frequently with no significant function in the story. Her habit of filling her letters with long, beautiful pictures of the Maine woods, of scenes "most touching and simple and curiously *archaic*",[84] carried over into her fiction. Many of her stories are so slightly plotted that it is impossible to analyze precisely the functions of their settings in terms of narrative structure.

"The Brandon House", which appeared in Jewett's first volume, *Deephaven* (1877), includes this colorful, but incidental, sunset picture-work:

the sea all around us caught the color of the clouds and though the glory was wonderful, I remember best one still evening when there was a bank of heavy gray clouds in the west shutting down like a curtain, and the sea was silver-colored. You could look under and beyond the curtains of clouds into the clearest yellow sky. There was a little black boat in the distance drifting slowly, climbing one white wave after another, as if it were bound into that other world beyond.[85]

A scene in bright red, white, and green is to be found in "Lady Ferry", printed in *Old Friends and New* (1879):

[81] Edward M. Chapman, "The New England of Sarah Orne Jewett", *Yale Review*, n. s., III, 162 (October, 1913), 160-61.
[82] See Matthiessen, *Sarah Orne Jewett*, 90.
[83] Pattee, *American Short Story*, 261.
[84] *Letters of Sarah Orne Jewett*, ed. Annie Fields (Boston and New York, 1911), 71.
[85] Sarah Orne Jewett, *Deephaven* (Boston and New York, 1919), 39.

[The house] was very large and irregular, with great white chimneys; and, while the river was all in shadow, the upper windows of two high gables were catching the last red glow of the sun. On the opposite side of a green from the house were the farm-house and buildings; and the green sloped down to the water, where there was a wharf and an ancient-looking storehouse.... And I saw a flock of white geese march solemnly up toward the barns. From the open green I could see that a road went up the hill beyond. The trees in the garden and orchard were richest green; their round tops were clustered thick together; and there were some royal great elms near the house. The fiery red faded from the high windows as we came near the shore.[86]

Still more frankly picturesque is this brief scene from "A Winter Drive", which appeared first in *Country By-Ways* (1881):

I noticed the bits of bright color against the dull green of the woods and the whiteness of the snow. The choppers wore red shirts and sometimes blue overalls, and there was a much-worn brown cap, with long ear-pieces.[87]

"Farmer Finch", in *Harper's* for January, 1885, boasts a picture that is literally splashed with colors:

now that it had sunk below the clouds, and in these late golden rays the barberry bush had taken on a great splendor.[88]

On the opening page of "Marsh Rosemary", in *The Atlantic Monthly* for May, 1886, Jewett's fondness for landscape paintings creeps in:

Ashore, the flaring light of the sun brought out the fine, clear colors of the level landscape. The marsh grasses were a more vivid green than usual, the brown tops of those that were beginning to go to seed looked almost red, and the soil at the edges of the tide inlets seemed to be melting into a black, pitchy substance like the dark pigments on a painter's palette.[89]

Innumerable examples of this kind of ornamentation are found in her stories, especially those included in *A White Heron and Other Stories* (1886), which were run in *Harper's* and the *Atlantic* during 1885 and 1886. By this time color-painting in descriptive setting

[86] Sarah Orne Jewett, *Old Friends and New* (Boston and New York, 1907), 183.
[87] Sarah Orne Jewett, *Country By-Ways* (Boston and New York, 1881), 182.
[88] Sarah Orne Jewett, *A White Heron and Other Stories* (Boston and New York, 1914), 40.
[89] Ibid., 86-87.

was a definite literary habit with Jewett, afterwards controlled rather successfully but never completely conquered.

The tendency to catalogue fauna and flora also marks some of her descriptive settings as conventional local color, though she is not nearly so immoderate in this respect as Cable and other Southerners. In one of the early *Deephaven* sketches, "In Shadow", an example of the opulence of New England nature may be found:

We saw a sleepy little owl on the dead branch of a pine tree; we saw a rabbit cross the road and disappear in a clump of juniper, and squirrels run up and down trees and along the stone-walls with acorns in their mouths. We passed straggling thickets of the upland sumach, leafless, and holding high their ungainly spikes of red berries; there were sturdy barberry-bushes along the lonely wayside, their unpicked fruit hanging in brilliant clusters. The blueberry-bushes made patches of dull red along the hillsides.[90]

The garden scene with a catalogue of flowers is rather common. In "A Lost Lover", in the *Atlantic* for March, 1878, there is a typical New England garden

with its herb-bed and its broken row of currant bushes, its tall stalks of white lilies and its wandering rose-bushes and honeysuckles, that bloomed beside the straight paths.[91]

In "Lady Ferry", in *Old Friends and New* (1879), there is a rather frayed garden, where, the narrator tells us,

I could hardly trace the walks, all over-grown with thick, short grass, though there were a few ragged lines of box, and some old rose-bushes; and I saw the very last of the flowers, – a bright red poppy, which had bloomed under a lilac-tree among the weeds.[92]

In "A Bit of a Shore Life", in the *Atlantic* for August, 1879, a more typical, pretty garden is described –

a gorgeous little garden to look at, with its red poppies, and blue larkspur, and yellow marigolds, and old-fashioned sweet, straying things, – all growing together in a tangle of which my friend seemed ashamed.[93]

In "The White Rose Road", in the *Atlantic* for September, 1889, the landscape

---

[90] *Deephaven*, 209-210.
[91] *Old Friends and New*, 16-17.
[92] Ibid., 225.
[93] Ibid., 264.

was a country of wild flowers; the last of the columbines were clinging to the hill-sides; down in the small, fenced meadows belonging to the farm were meadow rue just coming in flower, and red and white clover; the golden buttercups were thicker than the grass, while many mulleins were standing straight and slender among the pine stumps, with their first blossoms atop. Rudbeckias had found their way in, and appeared more than ever like bold foreigners.[94]

Perhaps more frequently than flowers Jewett sets forth a catalogue of trees, fir, spruce, pine, and cedar, but they are so much alive to her that she invariably personifies them and lends them a minor, or even major, role in the story. For this reason her finest trees seldom appear as mere background and ornament. If so, they are sketched only briefly, as if casually noticed in passing, as in this selection from "Mrs. Bonny" of the *Deephaven* collection:

Deephaven looked insignificant from that height and distance, and indeed the country seemed to be mostly covered with pointed tops of pines and spruces, and there were long tracts of maple and beech woods with their coloring of lighter, fresher green.[95]

After the first few series of stories, the long catalogue becomes less and less in evidence as a part of Jewett's technique. She never ceased to take her backgrounds seriously, but after some experimentation she began to weave them into her stories, so as to give them an even, woodsy atmosphere, rather than to paint them out on large canvases. In her masterpiece collection, *The Country of the Pointed Firs* (1896), "the scattered bits of description", so Shackford thinks, "give one the very look of green pastures, the scent of aromatic herbs, the fragrance of the sun-smitten spruce-trees, the sting of cool salt air, and the milder aspects of blue, sunshiny, safe harbors".[96] By 1896 she had learned the superiority of developing her setting chiefly by brief suggestion and implication rather than by lengthy, continuous descriptions. Another important fact is that at the same time her method was changing in this way, her awareness of nature as a living thing was affecting her whole attitude and feeling toward her raw materials.

[94] Sarah Orne Jewett, *Strangers and Wayfarers* (Boston and New York, 1896), 267-68.
[95] *Deephaven*, 192.
[96] Martha Hale Shackford, "Sarah Orne Jewett", *Sewanee Review*, XXX, 24 (January, 1922).

Mary E. Wilkins Freeman departed considerably from her sister-New Englander in her use of fictional setting for background and ornament. Freeman's atmosphere of decay and squalor stands in contrast with Jewett's affirmative attitudes; Freeman's restrained manner sets her far apart from Jewett with her ebullience and fluency. Freeman's general lack of ornamental setting and her emphasis on character and dramatic action are notably in contrast to Jewett's dramatic weakness and her sensitive preoccupation with landscape.

In Freeman's first two volumes of stories, decorative descriptive settings are conspicuously absent. Curiously enough, the earliest story now available, "Two Old Lovers", written before her father's death in 1883 and accepted by *Harper's Bazaar*, opens with two and a half pages devoted to describing the setting, but this device is dispensed with in "A Humble Romance", the second story, published in *Harper's Monthly* for June, 1884. Despite the fact that the main characters in this story roam through the country in a tin cart to peddle their wares, there is not one sentence descriptive of landscape until the very last page: "golden flecks of light sifted down on them through the rustling maple and locust boughs" while "the horse, with bent head, was cropping the tender young grass at the side of the road".[97]

Among the remaining twenty-six stories in the first volume, *A Humble Romance and Other Stories* (1887), there are several domestic exteriors used initially, the most pretentious of which include the following:

The first object in Ware, outside of my immediate personal surroundings, which arrested my attention was Munson house. When I looked out of my window the next morning it loomed up directly opposite, across the road, dark and moist from the rain of the night before. There were so many elm-trees in front of it and in front of the house I was in, that the little pools of rain-water, still standing in the road here and there, did not glisten and shine at all, although the sun was bright and quite high. The house itself stood back far enough to allow of a good square yard in front, and was raised from the street-level the height of a face-wall. Three or four steps led up to the front walk. On each side of the steps, growing near the edge of the wall, was an enormous lilac-tree in full blossom. I could see them tossing

[97] Mary E. Wilkins, *A Humble Romance and Other Stories* (New York, 1915), 24.

their purple clusters between the elm branches: there was quite a wind blowing that morning. A hedge of lilacs, kept low by constant cropping, began at the blooming lilac-trees, and reached around the rest of the yard, at the top of the face wall. The yard was gay with flowers, laid out in fantastic little beds, all bordered trimly with box. The house was one of those square, solid, white-painted, green-blinded edifices which marked the wealth and importance of the dweller therein half a century or so ago, and still cast a dim halo of respect over his memory. It had no beauty in itself, being boldly plain and glaring, like all of its kind; but the green waving boughs of the elms and the lilacs and the undulating shadows they cast toned it down, and gave it an air of coolness and quiet and lonely reserve.[98]

The long, low, red-painted cottage was raised above the level of the street, upon an embankment separated into two terraces. They were covered with green, slimy moss, and little ferns and weeds sprang out of every crack. A wall of flat slate stones led from them to the front door, which was painted green, sagged on its hinges, and had a brass knocker.

The whole yard and the double banks were covered with a tall waving crop of red-top and herds-grass and red and white clover. It was in the height of haying time.

A grassy wheel track led round the side of the house to a barn dashed with streaks of red paint.

Off to the left stretched some waving pasture land, and a garden patch marked by bean-poles and glancing corn blades, with a long row of beehives showing in the midst of it.[99]

Most of Freeman's houses are modest cottages, and her descriptions dwindle in proportion, as these more typical examples indicate:

The cottage house had been painted white, but the paint was now only a film in some places. One could see the gray wood through it. The establishment had a generally declining look; the shingles were scaling from the roof, the fences were leaning. All the bit of newness and smartness about it was the front door. That was painted a bright blue.[100]

This was a tiny white-painted house, with a door and one window in front, and a little piazza, over which the roof jutted, and over which the kitchen door opened, on the rear corner. The squashes were piled upon this piazza in a great yellow and green heap.[101]

Esther Gray's house was little and square, and mounted on posts like stilts. A stair led up to the door on the left side. Morning-glories climbed up the

[98] Ibid., 37-38.
[99] Ibid., 92.
[100] Ibid., 164.
[101] Ibid., 266.

stair-railing, the front of the house and the other side were covered with them, all the windows but one were curtained and matted with green vines.[102]

Aside from initial descriptions of village cottages, Freeman in her early stories practically limits her outside settings to domestic flowers and flower gardens. She is as delicate in her descriptions as though she were handling the posies and vignettes themselves – as though these plants were the only source of color and beauty in New England life. A few typical descriptions are the following:

The beds were laid out artistically in triangles, hearts, and rounds, and edged with box; boy's love, sweet williams, and pinks were the fashionable and prevailing flowers.[103]

Cinnamon rose-bushes grew in the square front yard. They were full of their little, sweet, ragged roses now. With their silent, lowly persistency they had overrun the whole yard. There was no stepping between them. They formed a green bank against the house walls; their branches reached droopingly across the front walk, and pushed through the fence.[104]

The morning-glories on the house were beautiful this morning, the purple and white and rosy ones stood out with a soft crispness.[105]

The dahlias were in full bloom, and they nodded their golden and red balls gently when the child jostled them. Beyond the dahlias on either side were zinnias and candy tuft and marigolds.[106]

Around the Caldwell house it [the air] was spicy sweet with pinks; there was a great bed of them at the foot of the green bank which extended under the front windows.[107]

In Freeman's second volume, *A New England Nun and Other Stories* (1891), there is a small increase in descriptive settings in both length and variety, though there is yet much evidence of a rigid economy in diction. A slight influence of the local color style, which had attained its height about 1884, is apparent in several stories of this volume. The title story of the collection boasts an "atmospheric" introduction:

It was late in the afternoon, and the light was waning. There was a difference in the looks of the tree shadows out in the yard. Somewhere in the

[102] Ibid., 296.
[103] Ibid., 23.
[104] Ibid., 164.
[105] Ibid., 299.
[106] Ibid., 399.
[107] Ibid., 415.

distance cows were lowing and a little bell was tinkling, now and then a farm-wagon tilted by, and the dust flew; some blue-shirted laborers with shovels over their shoulders plodded past; little swarms of flies were dancing up and down before the people's faces in the soft air. There seemed to be a gentle stir arising over everything for the mere sake of subsidence – a very premonition of rest and hush and night.[108]

Conventional color work appears in the picturization of a surreptitious love scene in the same story:

There was a full moon that night.... There were harvest-fields on either hand, bordered by low stone walls. Luxurious clumps of bushes grew beside the intervals.... Tall shrubs of blueberry and meadowsweet, all woven together and tangled with blackberry vines and horsebriers, shut her [Louisa] in on either side.... Opposite her, on the other side of the road, was a spreading tree; the moon shone between its boughs, and the leaves twinkled like silver. The road was bespread with a beautiful shifting dapple of silver and shadow; the air was full of mysterious sweetness.[109]

Incidental, but none the less picturesque, landscapes may be quoted almost at random:

In the morning it was very clear and cold, and there was the hard glitter of ice over everything. The snow crust had a thin coat of ice, and all the open fields shone and flashed. The tree boughs and trunks, and all the little twigs, were enamelled with ice. The roads were glare and slippery with it, and so were the door yards.[110]

Over his [Jonas's] head stretched the icy cherry-branches, full of the flicker and dazzle of diamonds. A woodpecker flew into the tree and began tapping at the trunk, but the ice enamel was so hard that he could not get any food.... Over in the east arose the mountain, covered with frosty foliage full of silver and blue and diamond lights.... Old Jonas paid no attention to anything.[111]

The moon came up over the mountain, and suddenly shadows of the trees grew darker and more distinct. There were four great elm-trees in the Amesbury yard. Over across the yard was a cemetery; back of that flowed the river; on the opposite bank of the river arose the mountain. The mountain was wooded to its summit. There were patches of silver on it, where some of the tree-tops waved in the moonlight.[112]

[108] Mary E. Wilkins Freeman, *A New England Nun and Other Stories* (New York, 1919), 1.
[109] Ibid., 12-13.
[110] Ibid., 160.
[111] Ibid., 162-63.
[112] Ibid., 178.

The snow creaked underfoot, the air was full of sparkles, there were noises like guns in the woods, for the trees were almost freezing. The moon was full, and seemed like a very fire of death, radiating cold instead of heat.[113]

The evergreen branches hung lower than ever; the snowflakes softly bent down the long slim sprays of the grave-yard bushes until they lay on the ground; the mildewed fronts of the slanting old grave-stones were hung with irregular, shifting snow-garlands.[114]

Though such examples may not reveal what Mary Moss calls Freeman's "deep sentient familiarity with the ways of nature",[115] they at least tend to refute Pattee's generalization that in her early period "her backgrounds are meager; the human element alone interests her".[116]

In the later nineties, after Freeman had become "sophisticated and self-conscious"[117] and "too much aware of herself as a literary person",[118] in the opinion of most critics she began to relax her rigid technique and to employ ornamentation with less discrimination. "The little Maid at the Door", included in *Silence and Other Stories* (1898), has this purely incidental landscape, toward which the characters are oblivious:

May was nearly gone; the pinks and the blackberry vines were in flower. All the woods were full of an indefinite and composite fragrance, made up of the breaths of myriads of green plants and seen and unseen blossoms, like a very bouquet of spring. The newly leaved trees cast shadows that were as much a part of the tender surprise of the spring as the new flowers. They flickered delicately before Joseph Baley and his wife Ann on the grassy ridges of the road, but they did not remark them.[119]

"The Tree of Knowledge", in *The Love of Parson Lord and Other Stories* (1900), contains this colorful spectacle:

It was a clear December night; there was no snow on the ground and the sun was setting redly. The limbs of the tree, with their mottle of red lichen,

[113] Ibid., 224.
[114] Ibid., 263.
[115] Mary Moss, "Some Representative American Story Tellers", *The Bookman*, XXIV, 28 (September, 1906).
[116] Pattee, *American Literature Since 1870*, 239.
[117] Ibid., 239.
[118] John Macy, "The Passing of the Yankee", *The Bookman*, LXXIII, 617 (August, 1931).
[119] Mary E. Wilkins, *Silence and Other Stories* (New York, 1898), 225.

reflected orange tints of flames, and looked like mottled orange snakes up-rearing in triangular contortions against the sky.[120]

From "The Cat", in *Understudies* (1901), comes this bright land-scape:

The trees rustle with a new sound to the spring wind; there was a flush of rose and golf-green on the breasting surface of a distant mountain seen through an opening in the wood. The tips of the branches were swollen and glistening red, and now and then there was a flower; but the cat had nothing to do with flowers.[121]

In the opening scene of "The Fair Lavinia", in *The Fair Lavinia and Others* (1907), may be seen as a complete abandonment on the part of Freeman to the nature school of story writing:

One looking from his window saw leaves of maples deepening from rose to green against the fixed green of others which had more direct sunlight. The dark limbs of oaks having dropped their last year's shag of russet, which had endured so long upon their knotty knees, to be pierced by violets and spring beauties, showed tufts of gold. Between the greens, ranging in all tones, were the cherry boughs, so aerial with white blooms that it seemed as if they might float away into space, and the slowly deepening gray and rose and white of the apple-trees. The lilacs were tipped with brown-ish pink; the snowball-bushes bore faint green spheres; the birches were clad as lightly as nymphs, revealing their graceful limbs, white with the passion of the spring, through dim clouds of amber green; the willows wept with tears of liquid gold, and everywhere were the gold bosses of the dandelions upon the green shield of spring.[122]

It was not by an abrupt change, but by a slow evolutionary development that Freeman gave up her earlier story formula, according to which setting was the merest domestic background, and began to ally herself in the late nineties and nineteen hundreds with the nature movement led by Cable, Allen, Murfree, and Jewett.

Turning to Edward Eggleston in the Middle West, the reader finds little innovation in the use of setting ornamentation. Despite the fact that Eggleston seems to have been interested in landscapes, regarding them as one of the formative influences in his own life; despite the fact that he showed an awareness of the importance of

---

[120] Mary E. Wilkins, *The Love of Parson Lord* (New York, 1900), 139.
[121] Mary E. Wilkins, *Understudies* (New York, 1901), 13.
[122] Mary E. Wilkins Freeman, *The Fair Lavinia and Others* (New York, 1907), 3-4.

an accurate setting by his comments on that subject; and despite the fact that description is one of his strongest points, a study of Eggleston's use of ornamental settings reveals little originality. Eggleston's short fiction is limited mainly to the stories in *Duffels* (1893), most of which were run in *Scribner's Monthly*, later *The Century Magazine*, during the author's apprenticeship days. "Ben: A Story for May-Day" (May, 1871) contains the most elaborate setting of all Eggleston's short stories. It abounds with May-Day spectacle, as the following landscape will illustrate:

After a while the wind lifted the fog that rested on the landscape, rolling it up like a curtain, disclosing the green pasture and the brook, the leafy trees on the southern exposure of the Indiana hills, the freshly plowed corn-fields, "the beautiful river", margined here and there with lofty white-and-green-trunked sycamores, and beyond the river the Kentucky hills, their cold northern slopes not yet much touched with vernal influences. And right in the valley on the Indiana side, and on the upper terrace of the level ground, lay the beautiful village of New Geneva, with its two or three mills, its vine-covered cottages, its yards full of trees, and the native vine-yards that had been planted by its first settlers, who were Swiss.[123]

The background of "Priscilla", which appeared in *Scribner's Monthly* for November, 1871, is the same little Swiss settlement in southern Indiana, where

the sweet air [is] perfumed with the blossoms of a thousand apple trees. For what yard is there in New Geneva that has not apple trees and grape-vines? And every family in the village keeps a cow, and every cow wears a bell, and every bell is on a different key.[124]

The Methodist church which Priscilla attends

had neither steeple nor bell nor anything churchlike about it except the two arched front windows. There was not even a fence to enclose it, nor an evergreen nor an ivy about it; only a few straggling black locusts.[125]

"Sister Tabea", the first story in *Duffels* (1893), offered a rather conventional, labored initial description of the setting:

Two weather-beaten stone buildings at Ephrata, in Pennsylvania, remain as monuments on this side of the water of the great pietistic movement in

---

[123] "Ben: A Story for May-Day", *Scribner's Monthly*, II, 72 (May, 1871).
[124] *Duffels*, 161.
[125] Ibid., 162.

Germany in the early part of the eighteenth century. One of these was called Rethanz, the other Sharon. A hundred and thirty or forty years ago there were other buildings with these, and the softening hand of time had not yet touched any of them. The door-ways were then, as now, on the ground level, the passages were just as narrow as dusky, the cells had the same little square windows to let in the day. But the stones in that day had a hue that reminded one of the quarry, the mortar between them was fresh, the shingles in the roof had gathered no moss and very little weather stain; the primeval forests were yet within the horizon, and there was everywhere an air of newness, of advancement, and of prosperity about Dunkard Convent.[126]

The convent fails not only in atmospheric interest, but also in producing an effect upon the characters. The author cannot avoid expositions of the activities of the inmates, though the convent is not again seen or felt by the reader. The environment exerts no apparent force upon Sister Tabea's mind.

The second story of the collection, "The Redemptioneer, A Story in Three Scenes", published in *The Century* for August, 1893, imitates the form of the drama in its formal statement of time and place at the beginning of each scene, a device used for satirical purposes in Mark Twain's "A Double Barreled Detective Story". Sanford Browne may glance eastward, "where the widening Potomac spread itself between low-lying bands, with never a brown hill to break the low horizon line",[127] or "where the green-blue water of the wide estuary melted into the blue-green of the sky with hardly a line of demarcation",[128] but the background has little individuality. There is an occasional picture, such as the following:

It was pretty to see the sloop heel over under a beam wind and shoot steadily forward, while the waves dashed fair against her weather side and splashed the water from time to time to the top of her free board. It was a pleasant sight to mark her approach by the gradual increase in her size and the growing distinctness with which the details of her rigging could be made out.[129]

[126] Ibid., 1.
[127] Ibid., 28-29.
[128] Ibid., 36.
[129] Ibid., 64-65.

But nothing in this ornament reinforces the dominant tone of the story, a tale of hate and vengeance and bitter memories.

"A Basement Story", like "Sister Tabea", is provided with a full initial but incidental description. The style exhibits a rhetorical tendency not characteristic of Eggleston's usual work:

There was no sun, and yet no visible cloud; there was nothing, indeed, to test the vision by; there was no apparent fog, but sight was soon lost in a hazy indefiniteness. Near objects stood out with a distinctness almost startling.... In the total absence of sky and the entire abolition of horizon the eye rejoiced, like Noah's dove, to find some place of rest; and the mainsail, smoky like the air, but cutting the smoky air with a sharp plane, was such a resting place for the vision. This sail and the reeky smokestack beyond, and the great near billows that emerged from time to time out of the gray obscurity – these seemed to save the universe from chaos.[130]

In most of Eggleston's stories the descriptive passages are brief and generalized. The words "beautiful" and "paradise" are much in evidence, as shown in the following examples:

If you would like to see some beautiful scenery, take a canoe and float down the Pomme de Terre River.[131]

There never was a more beautiful landscape than that which Lindsleyville commanded.[132]

That was long before the great tide of immigrants had begun to find their way into this paradise.[133]

Then the old farm seemed a sort of paradise.[134]

He stood upon the hillside overlooking the beautiful Ohio River.[135]

Hamlin Garland's treatment of setting, in view of his own well-expounded theory and the critical judgments that have been rendered on his radicalism, is somewhat surprising. Critics call attention to Garland's personal distaste for rural surroundings, to his representation of dirty cow lots and ugly, unpainted houses, but do not notice, for the most part, that his larger landscapes of

[130] Ibid., 64-65.
[131] Ibid., 91.
[132] Ibid., 92.
[133] Ibid., 92.
[134] Ibid., 213.
[135] *The Schoolmaster's Stories*, 63.

trees, clouds, and colored sunsets are generally magnificently decorative, and that they serve an important purpose in his literary
technique. It is true that Garland was, according to his own statement, "in no sense a naturalist"; yet, being a good friend of John
Burroughs, he "was moved to take a hand" in his friend's quarrel
with the "Nature-fakers".[136] "Birds and trees and waterfalls", he
tells us humorously in a later article, "are all very well, provided
they are taken in short vacations or by way of Sunday excursions,
when everybody is out of town and there is no mail".[137] In spite
of this attitude, however, one has not far to look in any of Garland's
descriptive or narrative writings to find scenes of great aesthetic
charm. In an essay for *Country Life in America* he reports that the
upper Mississippi River gave him

an impression of glorious color, of profound silence, of majestic loveliness
and of dream. It was all so solemnly beautiful by night, so gleaming, and
purple and empty by day. The stark high headlands looping away into
haze, the golden bars of sand jutting out into the burnished flood, the
thickets of yellow-green willows, the splendid oaks of bottom lands, the
little glades opening away to the hills, all suggested the time when the
red man's teepee and the red man's canoe were the only signs of man.[138]

He describes autumn trees which would "cause the heart of the
painter to ache with their loveliness".[139] Ruth M. Raw has observed that *A Son of the Middle Border* is filled with handsome pictures, and

tells of a bright world vanished, a landscape so beautiful that it hurt him to
have some parts of it revealed to aliens. At every step, in his description of
the terrible toil of the people, the beauty of the natural scene remains. He
makes us live the farm life of the Middle Border as he lived it, not only in
its squalor and ugliness and misery, but also in its wild beauty and glory.[140]

But no one has yet pointed out the large amount of aesthetic

[136] Hamlin Garland, "My Friend John Burroughs", *The Century Magazine*, CII,
737 (September, 1921).
[137] "Pioneers and City Dwellers", 372.
[138] Hamlin Garland, "The Middle West – Heart of the Country", *Country Life in
America*, XXII, 44 (September 15, 1912).
[139] Ibid., 24.
[140] Raw, op. cit., 202.

landscaping in *Main-Travelled Roads* (1891) and its companion volume, *Other Main-Travelled Roads* (1892).

For the most part, Garland's settings are too significant to be classified as background and ornament. In keeping with his own rule forbidding local color for its own sake, his backgrounds are generally represented as a part of a cosmic system incorporating both man and environment, as an influence upon the emotions or actions of characters, as a foil to the unaesthetic aspects of human life. Seldom, if ever, is his scenery purely incidental, or wholly for decoration. It is possible, however, to see in his tendency to set his characters in interesting poses and in colorful surroundings a definite link with the more conventional local colorists. In the following selections the scenes are arrested pictures pointing less directly to the characters than is usual in Garland's work:

This scene, one of the jolliest and most sociable of the Western farm, had a charm quite aside from human companionship. The beautiful yellow straw entering the cylinder; the clear yellow-brown wheat pulsing out at the side; the broken straw, chaff, and dust puffing out on the great stacker; the cheery whistling and calling of the driver; the keen, crisp air, and the bright sun somehow weirdly suggestive of time.[141]

Over the western wall of the circling amphitheatre the sun was setting. A few scattered clouds were drifting in the west wind, their shadows sliding down the green and purple slopes. The dazzling sunlight flamed along the luscious velvety grass, and shot amid the rounded, distant purple peaks, and streame d in bars of gold snd crimson across the blue mist of the narrower upper coollies.[142]

The circling hills were the same, yet not the same, as at night, a cooler tenderer, more subdued cloak of color lay upon them. Far down the valley a cool, deep, impalpable, blue mist hung, beneath which one divined the river ran, under its elms and basswoods and wild grapevines. On the shaven slopes of the hill cattle and sheep were feeding, their cries and bells coming to the ear with a sweet suggestiveness. There was something immemorial in the sunny slopes dotted with red and brown and gray cattle.[143]

The scene was characteristically, wonderfully beautiful. It was about five o'clock in a day in late June, and the level plain was green and yellow, and infinite in reach as a sea; the lowering sun was casting over its distant swells

141 Hamlin Garland, *Main-Travelled Roads*, New Edition (New York and London, 1899), 14.
142 Ibid., 74-75.
143 Ibid., 90-91.

a faint impalpable mist, through which the breaking teams on the neighboring claims ploughed noiselessly, as figures in a dream.... No other climate, sky, plain, could produce the same unnamable weird charm. No tree to wave, no grass to rustle, scarcely a sound of domestic life; only the faint melancholy soughing of the wind in the short grass, and the voices of the wild things of the prairie.[144]

Morning dawned at last, slowly, with a pale yellow dome of light rising silently above the bluffs, which stand like some huge storm-devastated castle, just east of the city. Out of the left the great river swept on its massive yet silent way to the south. Bluejays called across the water from hillside to hillside through the clear, beautiful air, and hawks began to skim the tops of the hills.[145]

On every side the golden June sunshine fell, filling the valley from purple brim to purple brim. Down over the hill to the west the light poured, tangled and glowing in the plum and cherry trees, leaving the glistening grass spraying through the elms, and flinging streamers of pink across the shaven green slopes where the cattle fed.[146]

Even now, in winter, with yellow-brown and green cedars standing starkly upon their summits, these towers possessed a distinct charm, and in the early morning when the trees glistened with frost, or at evening when the white light of the sun was softened and violet shadows lay along the snow, the whole valley was a delight to the eye, full of distinct and lasting charm.[147]

It was mid-spring. Everywhere was the vivid green of the Wisconsin landscape; the slopes were like carefully tended lawns, without stumps or stones; the groves rose up the hills, pink and gray and green in softly rounded billows of cherry bloom and tender oak and elm foliage. Here and there under the forest tender plants and flowers had sprung up, slender and succulent like all productions of a rich and shadowed soil.[148]

Meanwhile a triumphant sunset was making the west one splendor of purple and orange and crimson, which came over the cool green rim of the pines like the *Valhalla March* in Wagner.[149]

He sat in the doorway in vast content, unmindful of the glory of color that filled the western sky, and the superb evening chorus of the prairie-chickens, holding conventions on every hillock.[150]

[144] Ibid., 134.
[145] Ibid., 172.
[146] Ibid., 322.
[147] Hamlin Garland, *Other Main-Travelled Roads* (New York and London, 1910), 164.
[148] Ibid., 231-32.
[149] Ibid., 282.
[150] *Prairie Folks*, 143.

This list could be extended indefinitely, for aesthetic landscaping is a regular part of Garland's style. Though he says that "for me the grime and the mud and the sweat exist" and "still form a large part of life on the farm", and "shall go in my stories in their proper proportions",[151] these repugnant features are not associated with nature, unless nature has been changed by humanity. The large sweeping prairies are always beautiful in Garland's stories; it is only the farmer himself, his clothing, his dirty barns, houses, and cow lots, and his hot, dusty fields that are unaesthetic. Whether stated or implied, the ugly, man-made rural scene stands in vigorous contrast to the colored forests and distant hillsides. Vast, virgin nature demonstrates that all life can and ought to be beautiful. Only the pitiful farmer's immediate surroundings are fraught with tragedy. A few close-up landscapes ranging in emotional tone from slight irksomeness to thorough depression may be cited:

A cornfield in July is a sultry place. The soil is hot and dry; the wind comes across the lazily murmuring leaves laden with a warm sickening smell drawn from the rapidly growing, broad-flung banners of the corn.[152]

The town drew in sight – a cluster of small frame houses and stores on the dry prairie beside a railway station. There were no trees yet which could be called shade trees. The pitilessly severe light of the sun flooded everything. A few teams were hitched about, and in the lee of the stores a few men could be seen seated comfortably, their broad hat-rims flopping up and down, their faces brown as leather.[153]

The yellow March sun lay powerfully on the bare Iowa prairie, where the ploughed fields were already turning warm and brown, and only here and there in a corner or on the north side of the fence did the sullen drifts remain, and they were so dark and low that they hardly appeared to break the mellow brown of the fields.[154]

A funeral is a depressing affair under the best circumstances, but a funeral in a lonely farmhouse in March, the roads full of slush, the ragged clouds leaping the sullen hills like eagles, is tragic.[155]

On every side were the evidences of a ruined forest land. A landscape of

---

[151] Hazard, op. cit., 263.
[152] *Main-Travelled Roads*, 146.
[153] Ibid., 251.
[154] *Other Main-Travelled Roads*, 3.
[155] Ibid., 263.

flat wastes, of thinned and burned and uprooted trees. A desolate and apparently useless land.

Here and there a sawmill stood gray and sagging, surrounded by little cabins of unpainted wood to testify to the time when great pines stood all about, and the ring of the swamper's axe was heard in the intervals of silence between the howls of a saw.

To the north the swells grew larger. Birch and tamarack swamps alternated with dry ridges on which an inferior pine still grew. The swamps were dense tangles of broken and up-rooted trees. Slender pike-like stumps and fire-devastated firs rose here and there, black and grim skeletons of trees.

It was a land that had been sheared by the axe, torn by the winds, and blasted by fire.[156]

There are ugliness and unpleasantness in scenes which bear the imprint of man's labor, but one does not meet the maximum squalor in Garland's stories except in the more domestic scenes, or the settings closely related to character.

The preceding review of local color fiction in which setting is used at the lowest level, as background and ornament, is a demonstration of failure more often than success. It is easy to see why Twain was prompted to satirize this device and why many discerning critics, on the basis of such failures, gave the pejorative meaning to the phrase "local color". Of the ten writers reviewed, only three – Cable, Page, and Jewett – did at least a part of their best work while employing setting as an independent aesthetic device. The fact that so many failed in their attempts to use this device, succumbing to the temptation to over-indulge, indicates that a high degree of restraint is required of the author. He must exercise such restraint and control that he will not distort the proportions of his narrative and distract the reader's attention from the story-line; at the same time he must know that his scene is sufficiently emotionally evocative to justify its space and, even more importantly, that it harmonizes appropriately with the emotional tone of the story. That Cable and Page, with their nostalgic Southern scenes, were able to do this, is a proof of their literary skill, as well as a demonstration of the richness in texture of the materials which they employed.

[156] Ibid., 265.

3

SETTING IN CLOSE RELATION TO CHARACTER

Though most of the local colorists failed artistically when they elaborated their settings at the background level, they were more successful when they found a way to integrate setting with character. Those writers who, under the influence of biological and social Darwinism, perceived nature as man's environment, had less difficulty, on the whole, in integrating the elements of their fiction. But there are many non-scientific as well as scientific ways of relating man and nature, and the local colorists, in their far-ranging experimentation, came forth with a great variety of artistic devices, some old and some extraordinarily inventive and effective.

Though Harte cannot properly be called a naturalist, he had a scientific way of viewing life. He would not have attributed all conduct to environmental conditions, however; he frequently asserted that men owe much to their surroundings, that in the harmony between a creature and its habits lies more than meets the eye. This conviction grew upon him during the nineties and occasionally crops out in the mouths of his characters. For example:

It must be the contact of the vulgar earth – this wretched, crackling material, and yet ungovernable and lawless earth – that so depraved them [the natives].[1]

Here was the old philosophy which accepted the prairie fire and cyclone, and survived them without advancement, yet without repining. Perhaps in different places and surroundings a submission so stoic might have impressed him; in gentlemen who tucked their dirty trousers in their muddy boots and lived only for the gold they dug, it did not seem to him heroic.[2]

Women prematurely aged by frontier drudgery and childbearing, girls

---

[1] "Through the Santa Clara Wheat" (1891), ibid., VI, 341.
[2] "When the Waters Were Up at Jules" (1899), ibid., VI, 341.

who had known only the rigors and pains of a half-equipped, ill-nourished youth in their battling with the hard realities of nature around them.[3]

One scheme by which Harte has successfully linked setting with characters and their actions is to use particular natural objects or scenes as stimuli to bring about attitudes or feelings. There need be no concordance between scene and character based on past experience; the response elicited may be purely psychological. In such case the setting appears as a motivating influence on character.

That Harte was aware of the literary possibilities in this setting-character relation is evident. He was himself emotionally responsive to California landscapes, which "kept me in a state of excitement".[4] Likewise his characters are often emotionally aroused – sometimes even in a very emphatic way:

Again, when he [a lone pioneer in the Tules] essayed to bathe his parched and crackling limbs in its [the Sacramento's] flood, he would be confronted with the dazzling lights of the motionless steamboat and the glare of stony eyes – until he fled in aimless terror.[5]

As he rode abstractedly forward under the low cottonwood vault he felt a strange influence stealing over him, an influence that was not only a present experience, but at the same time a far-off memory.[6]

"I should be over the ledge before you came back! There's a dreadful fascination in it even now."[7]

He had swelled with strange emotions as he gazed at his ancestral hall.[8]

Not one of the stories from which these selections are drawn develops an important emotional response of characters to the setting. Suggestions of this kind usually turn out to be purely stylistic or literary. Though Harte's practice of alluding to the awe-inspiring quality of the scenery may not always be objectionable, it usually is when it is so prolonged as to constitute a false lead. For example, in "A Night on the Divide" (1898) a cultivated but colorless young woman finds herself alone for a short while in a snow-covered mountain range. Her reaction is profound:

[3] "An Esmeralda of Rocky Canon" (1899), ibid., XVI, 114.
[4] "How I Went to the Mines", ibid., XVIII, 253.
[5] "In the Tules" (1896), ibid., X, 390.
[6] "The Ancestors of Peter Atherly" (1898), ibid., XVI, 47.
[7] "A Jack and Jill of the Sierras" (1900), ibid., XVIII, 72.
[8] "A Romance of the Line" (1901), ibid., XVIII, 184.

The impressive and majestic solitude... seemed to descend upon her from the obscurity above. At first it was accompanied with a slight thrill of vague fear, but this passed presently into that profound peace which the mountains alone can give their lonely and perturbed children. It seemed to her that Nature was never the same, on the great plains where men and cities always loomed into such ridiculous proportions, as when the Great Mother raised herself to comfort them with smiling hillsides, or encompassed them and drew them closer in the loving arms of her mountains. The long white Canada stretched before her in a purity that did not seem of the earth; the vague bulk of the mountains rose on either side of her in a mystery that was not of this life. Yet it was not oppressive; neither were its restfulness and quiet suggestive of obliviousness and slumber; on the contrary, the highly rarefied air seemed to give additional keenness to her senses; her bearing had become singularly acute; her eyesight pierced the uttermost extremity of the gorge, lit by the full moon that occasionally shone through slowly drifting clouds. Her nerves thrilled with a delicious sense of freedom and a strange desire to run and climb.[9]

The reader who faithfully follows this character's emotional response afterward seeks in vain for its purpose in the story. The passage adds nothing to the individuality of the heroine, who turns out to be a mere sounding board. The quotation is more suggestive of travelogue than adventure.

In "Flip, a California Romance", the reaction of a stranger to the landscape is more adequately handled, and the setting takes on a function essential to the story. Lance Harriot, an exhausted fugitive, is "maddened and upheld" by the influence of a spicy wood until he can find assistance. He has wandered into a remote valley that is famed for its extraordinary power of inducing "the wildest exaltation" upon any "man and beast" who enters it.

The delicious spices of balm, bay, spruce, juniper, yerba buena, wild syringas, and strange aromatic herbs as yet unclassified, distilled and evaporated in that mighty heat, and seemed to fire with a mid-summer madness all who breathed their fumes. They stung, smarted, stimulated, intoxicated.

It was said that the most jaded and foot-sore horses became furious and ungovernable under their influences; wearied teamsters and muleteers, who had exhausted their profanity in this fiery air, extended their vocabulary, and created new and startling forms of objurgation.[10]

[9] *Writings*, XV, 292-93.
[10] Ibid., III, 295-96.

And in keeping with this legend, Harriot is made to experience a remarkable change of character. When he plunges into a stream for a bath, he enjoys a "startling transformation"; he not only washes himself, but "by the same operation" becomes "morally cleansed" of "every stain and ugly blot of his late misdeeds and reputation".[11] But Harriot's change is prolonged; when he leaves the valley he carries with him new ambitions and new purposes. The plausibility of the story aside, the point can be made from this example that setting can be successfully capitalized in a story, if its link with character is convincing.

Another way in which Harte sometimes integrates setting and character is by bringing persons into contact with natural phenomena in such a manner as to affect their aesthetic or moral nature, touching them physically, or altering their status in the world. A single natural object, a huge boulder situated near a mine, is portrayed with considerable detail in "A Millionaire of Rough and Ready" (1887).[12] Having discovered a rich vein of gold, a long-suffering prospector, Slinn, becomes paralyzed from shock as he waits for the coach beside the boulder marking the end of his claim and is unable to reveal his discovery. Years later his memory is revived by an accidental revisit to the same spot; but on a third visit to the locality he dies from shock and is unable to realize his hope of sudden riches.

"The Heritage of Dedlow Marsh" (1889) is the story of a young brother and sister struggling vainly to shake off the shackles of their narrow, dismal surrounding. Jim and Maggie have inherited from their eccentric father, Boone Culpepper, a vast tract of marshy land and a hatred for society. Long isolation at the old homestead has made these young people almost unsuitable for any other sort of life, as their stay at Logport proves to them. Logport society turns Jim into a frustrated lover and drunkard, driving him almost to suicide after the precedent of his father. Maggie blames her own ambitions for Jim's downfall; she should have known, she says,

---

[11] Ibid., 298.
[12] Ibid., V, 250 ff.

that there could be nothing in common between her folk [the family of Jim's lover] and such savages as we; that there was a gulf as wide as that Marsh and as black between our natures, our training and theirs; and even if they came to us across it, now and then, to suit their pleasure, light and easy as that tide – it was still there to some day ground and swamp them.[13]

"A Convert of the Mission" (1896)[14] is a good example of a character's adjustment to a new environment. A Protestant minister in poor health goes to a decadent Spanish town for a rest, where he becomes interested in a moonlit garden containing a beautiful senorita with a lovely voice. For a time he remains loyal to his own missionary instincts, but the whole spirit of the place so enthralls him that at last he becomes the convert, not the lady. A Catholic proselyte, he adopts the ways of the village and is found visiting the mission with his young lover. The motivation is skillfully handled, though the situations are artificial.

There is a suggestion of a third way in which setting has an influence upon characters in Harte's fiction, namely by representing to them a sign of Providence or a symbol of their own lives. This symbolic setting is not important or frequent enough in Harte's stories to deserve more than a mention, but it should not be overlooked. Though in none of Harte's stories is the setting as a whole symbolical, instances occur in which a particular scene symbolizes a general theme or truth to a particular character. The next-to-last scene[15] in "The Outcasts of Poker Flat", for example, in which the pure woman and the wicked are found lying peacefully side by side under a blanket of snow, seems to symbolize to the searching party – and the reader – the absurdity of conventional morality. Toward the end of "Miggles" (*Overland*, June, 1869), another of Harte's earliest stories, there is a striking tableau which reflects, at least to one of the travellers, the patience and self-sacrifice of the heroine for her paralyzed lover:

The storm had passed, the stars were shining, and through the shutterless window the full moon, lifting itself over the solemn pines without, looked into the room. It touched the lonely figure in the chair with an infinite

---

[13] Ibid., V, 449.
[14] Ibid., X, 281 ff.
[15] *Novels and Stories*, I, 35.

compassion, and seemed to baptize with a shining flood the lowly head of the woman whose hair, as in the sweet old story, bathed the feet of him she loved.[16]

In "Snow Bound at the Eagle's" the falling flakes of snow, Harte explains gratuitously, "seemed to illustrate the conviction that had been slowly shaping itself", namely, that all escape was blocked.[17] In "Jim's Big Brother from California" the stars, we read, "might have represented the extreme mutations in fortune in the settlement that night".[18] One more brief but rather effective touch of symbolism may be found in "The Reincarnation of Smith", wherein Smith, caught in an inextricable web of his own crimes and a hopeless love for a woman whom he has previously deserted as a wife, sees in a stream leading to the sea the only solution to his oppressive dilemma:

Yes [he muses], it was pointing him the only way out, – the path to the distant ocean and utter forgetfulness again![19]

And thus in the story the river, having flooded the country, carries his body out to the sea.

A fourth and last way in which Harte successfully worked out the idea of a fundamental character-environment connection was by the use of a person to embody the special characteristics of a locality, to represent, in a sense, the genius of a place. According to this scheme, the scene is partly represented by description, but its essential nature is further revealed by the person filled with its essence. Character and setting are thus mutually invigorated, each making the other more intelligible.

Such was the formula in Harte's first successful story. After the lame "My Metamorphosis" in April, 1868, there appeared in December of the same year one of the most original stories yet produced in this country, "The Work on Red Mountain". The central character, M'liss, a little waif as "shaggy as a Shetland colt and sleek-souled as little Eva",[20] is, to quote from Pattee,

[16] Ibid., I, 54-55.
[17] *Writings*, V, 161.
[18] Ibid., XVII, 104.
[19] Ibid., XVII, 299.
[20] Percy H. Boynton, *The Rediscovery of the Frontier* (Chicago, 1939), 74.

the incarnation of the wild lawlessness of a whole area, that primitive passion unchecked by convention and precedent, that irreverence and imperious self-assertion which had been born of the frontier and had culminated in the California of the gold-rush decade.... She had grown up untutored in the wild gulches of "Smith's Pocket" with men elemental in their hates and loves and appetites and ideal of freedom.[21]

M'liss is a strange product of a strange environment. She would be meaningless elsewhere, for Red Mountain is the key to her character; and the objects and scenes among which she lives gain in meaning because she is present to represent them. Harte must have felt that the favorable reception of this story was due to the strong local interest, for he rewrote it as a full-length serial three years later with even greater emphasis upon the locality. But the effort was a dismal failure, not because new material was added to expand it, but because, when he increased the bulk of the story, his erstwhile formula for connecting the setting to the character somehow escaped him.

With "Flip, a California Romance", the case is somewhat better. Flip, the central character, is less civilized even than M'liss, but is drawn along the same lines. "She was redolent of the spices of the thicket, and to the young man's excited fancy seemed at that moment to personify the perfume and intoxication of her native woods."[22] The tale rings surprisingly true for the most part, in spite of the unmistakable leanings toward cheap melodrama at the end. For Flip is unique, not beautiful. When Harte says in "A Maecenas of the Pacific Slope" (1891) that his heroine "standing there, graceful, glowing and animated,... looked the living genius of the recreated apartment",[23] he is using a mere figure of speech; but in "Flip" the girl and the spicy woods are by the force of repetition so completely fused that there can be no doubt of the connection.

One more example of this type will suffice. "A Sappho of Green Springs" (1891) is a story of a genuine local colorist, an anonymous poetess who has so perfectly reflected her natural surroundings that any one who knows the district well can find her exact locality

[21] Pattee, *American Short Story*, 230.
[22] *Writings*, III, 315.
[23] Ibid., VII, 370.

with no further information than that contained in her verse. She finds material even in "the little flicks and checkers o' light and shadder down in the brown dust".[24] Jack Hamlin, entering her particular valley, was sure at once that

this was the "underbrush" which the poet had described: the bloom above and below, the light that seemed blown through it like the wind, the suggestion of hidden life beneath this tangled luxuriance, which she alone had penetrated, – all this was here. But more than that, here was the atmosphere that she had breathed into the plaintive melody of her verse.[25]

As the story develops, the fact becomes clear that these particular woods and the poetess belong to each other and should never part. The character-setting link is fundamental in this story, not literary fancy. The story as a whole, however, is not efficiently shaped to bring it into full prominence.

From the foregoing examples, it is evident that Harte was experimenting with character-setting relationships in his stories. The failure of particular stories was sometimes a matter of shallowness of human interest, Dickensian sentimentality, or poor literary technique, but in many cases it can be traced to a malproportioned, discordant conjunction of setting with the other narrative elements, especially with his characters.

Harte's interpretation of the Western scene, viewed apart from his narrative art, aims in a general way to demonstrate its extraordinary aesthetic properties, to reveal the hazards and excitement under which its hardy inhabitants passed their lives without fear or perturbation, to illustrate the uncertainty of life and fortune in a land that is unknown and unpredictable. The Western environment, Harte seems to imply, has produced a stolid, stoical race, reckless in danger, unmindful of the sudden inversions of fortune, ridiculously rough in the exterior, but tender and sentimental in its interior aspects, however eccentric it appears to the uninitiated. The incongruity of a Westerner in another part of the world is a common motif among all of the local colorists of this section; and the titles of Harte's stories alone will reveal his special satirical

24 Ibid., VI, 405.
25 Ibid., 420.

delight in finding, among his own Sierras, a Western prototype for the personages of heroic antiquity and classical mythology.

The case was far different with a second Western local colorist, Mark Twain, who became in his later years thorougly mechanistic, as well as romantic, in his attitude toward life and human conduct. This dual outlook could, quite conceivably, have had a serious effect on his use of setting and character in his fiction. Always conscious of his own Western environment, he doubtless felt himself identified with it throughout his life. In several novels[26] he k ows himself to be more an environmentalist than hereditarian, and jokes about obscure parentage. But he was nevertheless skeptical about the possibility of real volition. In his essay "What is Man?" published anonymously in 1906, he speaks of "Man the machine – man the impersonal engine":

Whatsoever a man is, is due to his *make*, and to the *influences* brought to bear upon it by his heredities, his habitat, his associations. He is moved, directed, COMMANDED, by exterior influences – *solely*. He *originates* nothing, not even a thought.[27]

The view expressed in this quotation would lead one to expect more naturalism in Mark Twain's fiction than is actually to be found. In his earlier work, at least, determinism is not a significant factor in the character-setting relationships in his fiction.

"The Celebrated Jumping Frog of Calaveras County",[28] which immediately brought the author not only national but also international fame, is remarkably restrained in the use of setting. Does it have a real setting, and if so, what is its function? There is of course no scenery or spectacle; there is not one sentence in the entire story that brings to mind any object or picture that is uniquely Western, except, perhaps, for the mention of "the barroom stone of the dilapidated tavern in the decayed mining camp of Angels".[29] The setting is too fragmentary to make a visual impression upon the average reader; the only way in which the West as a vast background is realized is through the personality of Jim

---

[26] For example, *The Tragedy of Puddinhead Wilson*, 1894.
[27] *Works*, XIX, 5.
[28] *Saturday Press*, Nov. 18, 1865.
[29] Ibid., XVII, 17.

Smiley. As Smiley talks and goes calmly about his business of betting on things, there is an impression that he is certainly a product of a strange, free, raw, extravagant, and fun-loving world. Smiley is a kind of European ideal of American independence, and through his behavior the Western scene is figuratively represented. Thus in a literal sense the story has no setting beyond the most general and incidental indication of time and place; but in a more implicit way the West comes to light as the unique region to v .ch the story applies. The plot itself harks back to the remotest antiquity, but the real substance of the story, the speech, attitudes, and actions of Smiley are artistically and thoroughly localized. And since the main character is represented as a kind of person whom one might reasonably expect to find in the West, he is to that extent a Western type and may be considered, without stretching the point too far, as a device for representing the life of the particular county in which he lives. The story thus logically belongs to the body of local color literature.

The best example in all of Twain's work of a short story in which the setting is handled descriptively and made to function in a close relation to a character is "The Californian's Tale" (1893), which is, in fact, almost unique. It is the single example of a short story in which the reader's eye is actually trained on the landscape, and in which a scene is maintained long enough to make any real impression. And it is almost the only story in which description is used in a serious way for setting. The initial scene runs thus:

It was a lovely region, woodsy, balmy, delicious, and had once been populous, long years before, but now the people had vanished and the charming paradise was a solitude.... In one place, where a busy little city with banks and newspapers and fire companies and a mayor and aldermen had been, was nothing but a wide expanse of emerald turf, with not even the faintest sign that human life had ever been present there.[30]

This style, and especially the tone, is unusual in the short stories of Mark Twain. The descriptive manner suggests the travel-sketching of *Roughing It*. Advancing to the next scene, we find the dominant impression reiterated:

[30] Ibid., X, 184-85.

It was a lonesome land! Not a sound in all those peaceful expanses of grass and woods but the drowsy hum of insects; no glimpse of man or beast; nothing to keep up your spirits and make you glad to be alive.[31]

And, indeed, only in such a desolate country could things happen as they do in "The Californian's Tale". Perhaps nowhere else would a traveller be so much uplifted by his visit to a plain cottage, with a "garden of flowers, abundant, gay, and flourishing"[32] and with a modest interior revealing the hand of a woman, that he would prolong his visit for days. Nowhere else would a man be so likely to lose his mind through brooding loneliness for a lost wife. The whole story belongs to California and represents it. The pictures of the background come into the story not so much to operate anew upon the characters and influence them, for this effect has already been realized; it is chiefly to explain why they are as they are. A feeling of loneliness is also directly and independently communicated to the reader, but again the main function of the setting is to validate the whole story by making the behavior of Henry, the other Californian, and the narrator intelligible.

Both of these short stories, "Jumping Frog" and "Californian's Tale", are strongly localized, and each reveals a distinct aspect of Western life as the author knew it. Those aspects were vastly different and the narrative technique varies accordingly. In the first everything depends upon character and the manner of telling the story; in the second the style is almost formal and conventional and the total effect depends upon an artistic combination of all the usual elements – setting, character, and incident.

Though Cable, the first of the Southern group, usually keeps setting independent of character and plot, several of his stories depart from this procedure. Cable's characters are generally natives fully adapted to their surroundings, to which they are themselves emotionally insensible; it is therefore usually upon the outsiders that the landscapes and old houses make an impression. From Cable's strong religious bent one can infer that he did not believe in a mechanistic world with human beings the product of environmental forces. As the cure observes in "Caranco",

[31] Ibid., 185.
[32] Ibid., 188.

Some children [like 'Tanase] are born with fixed characters; you can tell almost from the start what they are going to be. Be they much or little, they are complete in themselves, and it makes comparatively little difference into what sort of a world you drop them.

But there is also, as represented in Bonaventure,

the other type; just as marked and positive traits, but those traits not yet builded into character: a loose mass of building-material, and the beauty or ugliness to which such a nature may arrive depends on who and what has the building of it into form. What he may turn out to be at last will be no mere product of circumstances; he is too original for that. Oh, he's a study! Another boy under the same circumstances might turn out entirely different; and yet it will make an immense difference how his experiences are allowed to combine with nature.[33]

For the cure, and for Cable, life is too complex to be resolved into causes and effects. Sometimes circumstance, or nature, seems to be an objective, purposeless influence, and sometimes it is a symbol or a tool employed by a Divine Power. The beauties and benevolence of nature are ordinarily assigned a potency that makes for morality in man. "O God", prays the priest in "Madame Delphine",

be very gentle with those children who would be nearer heaven this day had they never had a father and mother, but had got their religious training from such a sky and earth as we have in Louisiana this holy morning! Ah! my friends, nature is a big-print catechism.[34]

On the other hand, the malevolent aspects of nature, such as drouth and loss of lovers or property, are commonly associated with the voodoo curse and conspiracy with the Evil One. In "Au Large" (*Bonaventure*) is found Cable's most lucid commentary on man's relation to Nature:

Shall we ever subdue her and make her always submissive and compliant? Who knows? Who knows what man may do with her when once he has got self, the universal self, under perfect control? ...The very lions of Africa and the grizzlies of the Rockies, so they tell us, are no longer the bold enemies of man they once were. "Subdue the earth" – it is being done. Science and art, commerce and exploration, are but parts of religion. Help us, brothers all, with every possible discovery and invention to complete the conquest

---

[33] *Bonaventure*, 30.
[34] *Old Creole Days*, 21.

begun in that first garden whence man and woman first came forth, not for vengeance but for love, to bruise the serpent's head, but as yet, both within us and without us, what terrible revolts doth Nature make; what awful victories doth she serve over us, and then turn and bless and serve us again![35]

"Jean-Ah Poquelin" (1875) is the earliest story stressing environmental influences. The principal scene begins with a brooding, melancholy picture:

The house was of heavy cypress, lifted up on pillars, grim, solid, and spiritless, its massive build a strong reminder of days still earlier, when every man had been his own peace officer and the insurrection of the blacks a daily contingency. Its dark, weather-beaten roof and sides were hoisted up above the jungly plain in a distracted way, like a gigantic ammunition wagon stuck in the mud and abandoned by some retreating army. Around it was a dense growth of low water willows, with half a hundred sorts of thorny or fetid bushes, savage strangers alike to the "language of flowers" and to the botanist's Greek. They were hung with countless strands of discolored and prickly smilax, and the impassable mud below bristled with *chevaux de frise* of the dwarf palmetto. Two lone forest trees, dead cypresses, stood in the center of the marsh, dotted with roosting vultures. The shallow strips of water were hid by myriads of aquatic plants, under whose coarse and spiritless flowers, could one have seen it, was a harbor of reptiles, great and small, to make one shudder to the end of his days.

The house was on a slightly raised spot, the levee of a draining canal. The waters of this canal did not run; they crawled, and were full of big, ravenous fish and alligators, that held it against all comers.[36]

Since a suspicion of murder hung upon the myterious old hermit who inhabited this unhappy place, Cable explains that "the man and his house were alike shunned"; "that the snipe and duck hunters forsook the marsh, and the wood cutters abandoned the canal". For

Among both blacks and whites the house was the object of a thousand superstitions. Every midnight, they affirmed, the *feu follet* came out of the marsh and ran in and out of the rooms, flashing from window to window.... There was a bottomless well, everybody professed to know, beneath the sill of the big front door under the rotten veranda; whoever set his foot upon that threshold disappeared forever in the depth below.[37]

[35] *Bonaventure*, 291-92.
[36] *Old Creole Days*, 179-80.
[37] Ibid., 183-84.

And the evil influence of the place reached beyond its own area, withering crops and spreading misery.

"Bibi", a daring story which won Edward King's admiration in 1873 but was rejected by *Scribner's*, did not find a publisher until it was included in *The Grandissimes* in 1880 as "The Story of Bras-Coupe". Later it appeared as a short story in *The Cable Story Book* (1911). This tale, like the preceding one, makes generous use of the evil-curse motif; the landscape reacts to Bras-Coupe's influence rather than the reverse.

The plantation became an invalid camp. The words of the voudou found fulfilment on every side. The plow went not out; the herds wandered through broken hedges from field to field and came up with staring bones and shrunken sides; a frenzied mob of weeds and thorns wrestled and throttled each other in a struggle for standing-room – ragweed, smart-weed, sneeze-weed, bind weed, iron-weed – until the burning skies of midsummer checked their growth and crowned their unshorn tops with rank and dingy flowers.[38]

The *Bonaventure* stories, consisting of "Caranco", "Grande Pointe", and "Au Large", are set in the backwoods of Louisiana, chiefly along the bayous, lakes, swamps, and "shaking prairies". The settings include endless catalogues of swamp flora, with emphasis on strange specimens, but there is also something new in the way these settings are related to the characters. In "Caranco" (1887) there is an emphatic sensitivity of characters to the wild nature; the child-of-nature motif is worked out in the representation of the young Bonaventure, who "lay in ambush for butter-flies", and "came under the spell of marigolds, prince's feathers, lady-slippers, immortelles, portulaca, jonquil, lavender, althaea, love-apples, sage, violets, amaryllis, and that grass ribbon they call jarretiere de la vierge – the virgin's garter".[39] During his long search for 'Thanase he wanders through the swamps and fields until his "companioning with nature had browned his skin and dried his straight, fine hair".[40] Occasionally nature is a guide to him on his wanderings; once "the crescent moon ran before him in

---

[38] *The Cable Story Book* (New York, 1911), 54-55.
[39] *Bonaventure*, 7.
[40] Ibid., 49.

the sky, and one glowing star, dipping low, beckoned him into the west".[41] Many pictures, rivers "shining like a silken fabric in the sunset lights", "hillsides clad in crimson, green, and gold", "huge dazzling clouds moving like herds of white elephants pasturing across heavenly fields",[42] pass before the eyes of the vagabond. The theme of the story requires that his character be formed through such contacts.

"Grande Pointe" (1887) continues with Bonaventure's experiences, now as a backwoods schoolmaster in the sugar plantations. Entering the region as a novice, he is much impressed by the luxuriousness of the swamp ferns about his feet, and the goldenrod "of stature greater than his own". Sometimes he must "push apart the brake-canes and press through with bowed head".[43] The natives are so well adjusted to their surroundings that "their diffident gaze bore that look of wild innocence that belongs to those who see more of dumb nature than of men".[44] The most beautiful product that the prolix nature of Grande Pointe has produced is the little "'Cadian" maiden, Sidonie, a "wild rose-tree". Like M'liss in Harte's "The Work on Red Mountain", she is the genius of the region that has nurtured her, and can flourish only in her natural surroundings. "Mark you", says the author,

> this was in Grande Point. I have seen the wild flower taken from its cool haunt in the forest and planted in the glare of a city garden. Alas! the plight of it, poor outshone, wilting, odorless thing! And then I have seen it again in the forest; and pleasanter than to fill the lap with roses and tulips of the conservatory's blood-royal it was to find it there once more the simple queen of the queen solitude.[45]

So Sidonie.

The last of the *Bonaventure* series, "Au Large" (1887), assumes novelette proportions, dealing with the education and civilization of the *prairie tremblante* west of New Orleans. Unlike Sidonie in "Grande Pointe", the rustics in this story, most of whom are carried

[41] Ibid., 53.
[42] Ibid., 54.
[43] Ibid., 78.
[44] Ibid., 79.
[45] Ibid., 117.

over from the preceding story, leave their plantation homes and take up residence in the city. Young Marguerite retains

only so little rusticity as became itself a charm rather than a blemish, suggested the sugar-cane fields; the orange-grove; the plantation-house, with pillared porch, half-hidden in tall magnolias and laurustines and bushes of red and white camellias....[46]

So well does she learn to love New Orleans that her mother finally realizes "that her child could never come back to the old surroundings and be content.... What a change from the child that had left her! It was like a change from a leaf to a flower".[47] St. Pierre, in order to be near his son and yet retain his old connection with the forests, becomes "an operator in the wild products of the swamp, the *prairies tremblantes*, the lakes, and in the small harvest of the *pointes* and bayou margins: moss, saw-logs, venison, wild-duck, fish, crabs, shrimp, melons, garlic, oranges, Perique tobacco."[48]

In a later story, "The Solitary" (1896), Cable again deals with the problem of readjustment to a new environment. Disappearing from the city without a trace, Gregory sails unnoticed from the Delta to a small uninhabited island in the Gulf, destroys his boat, and begins a secluded life. To Gregory "this solitude brought no quick distress";[49] for him

There was an infinite relief merely in getting clean away from the huge world of men, with all its exactions and temptations and the myriad rebukes and rebuffs of its crass propriety and thrift. He had endured solitude enough in it; the secret loneliness of a spiritual bankruptcy.[50]

The effect of the new environment is spiritual revelation:

Skyward ponderings by night, canny discoveries under foot by day, quickened his mind and sight to vast and to minute significances, until they declared an Author known to him hitherto only by tradition.[51]

In the second week, however, the loneliness becomes unbearable. "Dawn widened over sky and sea, but its vast beauty only mocked

[46] Ibid., 205.
[47] Ibid., 237.
[48] Ibid., 251.
[49] *Strong Hearts* (New York, 1908), 23.
[50] Ibid., 25-26.
[51] Ibid., 26-27.

the castaway", who "wandered up and down and across his glittering prison". His body suffers from a lack of habitual stimulants, but more terrible than this is "the horror of his isolation growing – growing – like the monsters of his dream".[52] Failing to halt a passing vessel, he begins the construction of a raft, only to have it destroyed by a storm, the symbol of his own passion. When the tempest is over, "even more completely the tumult within him was quieted...."[53]

Murfree, in a number of her stories, experiments by changing the relationship between the character, whether native or outsider, and his mountain environment. Not acquainted with mountain life herself until she was twenty-three, she was never an expert on the manner of life in this region; yet, like Chevis in "The Star of the Valley", she seems to have obtained "a comprehensive idea of the machinery of life in the wilderness", and found it "more complicated than one could believe, looking upon the changeless face of the wide, unpopulated expanse of mountain ranges stretching so far beneath that infinite sky".[54] She did not ever completely master the mountain culture; she "looked upon these people and their inner life only as picturesque bits of the mental and moral landscape", unaware that it was only "an aesthetic and theoretical pleasure"[55] which they gave her.

Sometimes Murfree assumes, as in "The Dancin' Party at Harrison's Cove", that "human nature is everywhere the same", that mountaineers are merely human beings, that "the Wilkins settlement is a microcosm"[56] of universal society, irrespective of environmental variations. Sometimes the surrounding conditions play their part in shaping her characters. Rufus Chad of Big Injun Mounting, for example, has derived "from his rugged heights certain subtle native instincts".[57] Regardless of the relation between character and environment in a particular story, there is one fundamental idea running through all of the environmental

[52] Ibid., 27.
[53] Ibid., 38.
[54] *In the Tennessee Mountains*, 134.
[55] Ibid., 134-35.
[56] Ibid., 223.
[57] Ibid., 162.

stories: that is, the mountainous country itself is always of more importance than the creature inhabiting it at the present moment. "Humanity seemed so small, so transitory a thing", she wrote in "The Romance of Sunrise Rock", when it is compared with "the undying grandeur of the mountains. Material nature conquers; man and mind are as naught".[58] In "The Phantoms of the Foot-Bridge" (1895) a particularly impressive landscape is said to have

fostered a realization of the pitiable minuteness and helplessness of human nature in the midst of the vastness of inanimate nature and the evidences of infinite lengths of forgotten time, of the long reaches of unimagined history.[59]

All of Murfree's best stories reveal some kind of close connection, usually structural rather than emotional, between the setting of a story and the other elements.[60] Her uses of setting on this level include all of the types found in Harte's work: (1) as an emotional, aesthetic, or moral stimulus; (2) as an influence upon action; (3) as a symbol to a character; (4) as an environment reflected in a character, the genius of a place. But these fundamental setting-character relations are not the end of Murfree's efforts; they are merely the raw materials of more intricate and complex combinations of setting and character occurring in her better short stories.

Murfree's use of animate nature as an emotional and moral influence is well illustrated in "Electioneering on Big Injun Mounting" (1884), which has as its theme the influence of natural environment on moral character. Rufus Chadd, of Big Injun, has been elected state attorney. To use the author's words:

The mountaineer seemed to have brought from his rugged heights certain subtle native instincts, and the wily doublings of the fox, the sudden savage spring of the catamount, the deadly sinuous approach of the copperhead, were displayed with a frightful effect, translated into human antagonism – the juries fell under his domination, as the weak always submit to the strong.[61]

His former friends back home, who have misunderstood his mo-

[58] Ibid., 183.
[59] *The Phantoms of the Foot-Bridge and Other Stories* (New York, 1895), 16
[60] Cf. Richard Carey, *Mary N. Murfree* (New York, 1967), 47.
[61] *In the Tennessee Mountains*, 162.

tives, begin to feel that he has deserted them to enjoy the ease of town life. Chadd, weary of prejudice and hostility and accused of betraying his own people, seeks a solace in the haunts of his youth:

The calm of the woodland, the refreshing aromatic odors, the rising winds after the heat of the sultry day, exerted a revivifying influence upon the lawyer's spirits, as he walked on into the illimitable solitudes of the forest.[62]

The return-of-the-native motif offers ample opportunity for blending character and setting. In his story the hero, despite superficial changes, exhibits under a crucial test that generosity of spirit which characterizes all the true sons of Big Injun.

Sometimes with Murfree a particular scene, frequently a magnificent tableau, produces a change in the action of a character so pronounced as to constitute the turning point of a story. In several stories, for example, a Christmas tableau diverts a character's course of action. In " 'Way Down in Lonesome Cove" (1885) a potential murderer follows his victim into a dark cave, suddenly to behold a miracle:

A soft aureola with gleaming radiations, a low shadowy chamber, a beast feeding from a manger, and within it a child's golden head....[63]

The effect of this picture on the character is immediately perceptible:

With a thrill in his heart, on his knees he drew the charge from his rifle, and flung it down a rift in the rocks. "Christmas Eve", he murmured.[64]

A story in which the general surroundings rather than a particular scene produce important reactions in the characters is the "Romance of Sunrise Rock". Two outsiders, young men who have failed in their respective professions, are molded into new shapes by the unique forces of Sunrise Rock. But they do not react in the same manner. One cannot at first adapt himself:

He could not understand this world; he could not understand the waste of

[62] Ibid., 173.
[63] *The Phantoms of the Foot-Bridge*, 176.
[64] Idem.

himself and his friend in this useless, purposeless way; he could not even understand the magnificent waste of nature about him.[65]

Nevertheless his broken spirit is healed at Sunrise Rock, and he receives an impetus which enables him to succeed back in the professional world where he has previously failed. His companion, on the other hand, becomes thoroughly committed to mountain life, develops a new set of values, and comes permanently under the spell of his adopted home,

For the skepticism of his college days has fallen from him somehow, and his views have become primitive, like those of his primitive neighbors. There is a certain calm and strength in the old theories. With the dawn of a gentle and hopeful peace in his heart, very much like the comfort of religion, he goes his way in the misty moonrise.[66]

A story which makes a symbolic use of an inanimate natural object is "The Casting Vote" (1893). It begins with the appearance of a comet in the skies which comes to have many different meanings for the mountaineers – as for all peoples of all ages according to their own particular interests and prejudices. The sky has always been the proper place for symbols:

It is an open scroll, that magnificent, wonder-compelling cult of the skies, not the sealed book of the sciences. Since the days of the Chaldean, all men of receptive soul in solitary places, the sailor, the shepherd, the hunter or the hermit, whether of the wilderness of nature or the isolation of crowds, have read there of the mystery of the infinite, of the order and symmetry of the plan of creation, of the proof of the existence of a God....[67]

It is not surprising, therefore, that the superstitious natives of Kildeer County are trying to interpret this heavenly symbol while the minor events of the story unfold. As the title suggests, the story revolves around a deciding vote in a tied political race. "The castin' vote", remarks an observer, "is as *phee*-nomenal an' ez astonishin' ez the comet. Something like the comet, too; it has its place in the legal firmament, but 'taint often necessary to use it".[68] Thus the true meaning of the comet for Kildeer County is at last intimated.

[65] *In the Tennessee Mountains*, 203.
[66] Ibid., 213-14.
[67] *The Mystery of Witch-Face Mountain*, 250-51.
[68] Ibid., 20.

The sole example in all of Murfree's short stories of a character as the genius of a place is her "The Star in the Valley" (1878). Chevis, a hunter from the civilized world, perceives the "star" and wonders at it even before Hi Bates explains that " 'taint nuthin' but the light in Jerry Shar's house".[69] But it does not lose "its poetic aspect", for the next day the hunter becomes acquainted with Shaw's daughter, a shy little waif of the mountains, and "that night looked with a new interest at the red star, set like a jewel in floating mists of the valley".[70] Visiting the Shaws on the pretext of shoeing a horse, Chevis is able to gain a closer view of the little beauty, to whom "it seemed as if the wild nature about her had been generous". Her "opaline" eyes and "bronze hair" are tinted like sunset clouds; and

> there was a subtle affinity between her and other pliant, swaying, graceful young things, waving in the mountain breezes, fed by the rain and the dew. She was hardly more human to Chevis than certain lissome little woodland flowers, the very names of which he did not know, – pure white, star-shaped, with a faint green line threading its way through each of the five delicate petals.[71]

> He had been touched in a highly romantic way by the sweet beauty of this little woodland flower. It seemed hard that so perfect a thing of its kind should be wasted here, unseen by more appreciative eyes than those of bird, or rabbit, or the equally uncultured human beings around her.[72]

> He looked at it all from an ideal point of view. The star in the valley was only a brilliant set in the night landscape, and suggested a unique and pleasing experience.[73]

Julia Shaw epitomizes not only the physical beauty of the valley, but the moral splendors as well. Lonely and disappointed, she nevertheless sacrifices herself for a moral purpose with the quiet, uncomplaining heroism that characterizes all life in the valley, human and animal alike.

> There are many things that suffer unheeded in those mountains: the birds that freeze on the trees; the wounded deer that leaves its cruel kind to die

[69] *In the Tennessee Mountains*, 121.
[70] Ibid., 124.
[71] Ibid., 131.
[72] Ibid., 133.
[73] Ibid., 135.

alone; the despairing, flying fox with its pursuing train of savage dogs and men.... And the jutting crag whence had shone the camp-fire she had so often watched – her star, set forever – looked far over the valley beneath, wherein one of those sad little rural graveyards, she had been laid so long ago.[74]

There are other stories in which inanimate nature stands in close relation to character, but the connection is not so well maintained throughout the story as it is in the examples cited.

About ten of Page's sixty short stories have settings developed in close relation to character, but there is little variety in the nature of this relationship. There are a few suggestions of a setting revealed through character, as in "Elsket" (1891), in which "none but those who have Harold Hoarfager's blood" can pass "the narrow ledge and the Devil's Seat"[75] in a certain unexplored mountainous region; or in "A Soldier of the Empire" (1886), in which Camille, a flower of nature, "her cheeks as pink as the roses in the gardens of the Tuileries", cannot live for long away from her native Lorraine, for "the close walls of the city had not suited her, and she languished before his [her husband's] eyes like a plucked lily."[76] Page seems to have been far less concerned, as a usual thing, about environment than about heredity, which he took very seriously. Pattee has noticed that Page's heroes and heroines are thoroughbreds; their excellence of character is, to use the title of one of his stories, "bred in the bone". Another story, "Run to Seed" (1891), refutes the idea that good stock will lose its nobility because of impoverished circumstance or unwholesome companionships.

Only rarely, as in the early portion of "Little Darby", does Page assign much importance to environment as a force shaping humanity. In a remote and barren par⸴ of the Piedmont, the author explains, there was a forgotten settlement. "Possibly it was this poverty of the soil or unwholesomeness of their location, which more than anything else kept the people of this district somewhat distinct from others around them, however poor they might be."[77] Their blood was good, for "they had the names of the old English

[74] Ibid., 154.
[75] Elsket, and Other Stories (New York, 1894), 29.
[76] Ibid., 184-85.
[77] Burial of the Guns, 176.

gentry", and in their youth were "straight, supple, young fellows with clear-cut features, and lithe, willowy-looking girls, with pink faces and blue, or brown, or hazel eyes, and a mien which one might have expected to find in a hall rather than in a cabin". But in later life their hard environment began to take effect; "when they were bowing to middle age, their life told on them and made them weather-beaten and not infrequently hard-visaged."[78]

The usual way in which Page links environment with character in a story is to allow the character to react emotionally to a scene or some portion of it. In "The Burial of the Guns", for example,

the loneliness of the mountain seemed to oppress them; the mountains stretching up so brown and gray on one side of them, and so brown and gray on the other, with their bare, dark forests soughing from time to time as the wind swept up the pass. The minds of the men seemed to go back to the time when they were not so alone, but were part of a great and busy army.[79]

Aside from brief and incidental passages of this sort, almost all of Page's characters who are emotionally responsive to nature can be arranged into two groups: persons who have a superstitious fear of a particular place, usually a haunted house; and persons who find great aesthetic joy in the presence of landscape which is relatively new, and of which they have not become oblivious through long experience.

The haunted-house motif, already noticed in Cable's work, was a favorite among the Southern local colorists. Several of Page's stories, "Her Great-Grandmother's Ghost" (1894), "The Spectre in the Cart" (1904), and "Old 'Stracted" (1886), belong to this variety, but the earliest and by far the best example is "No Haid Pawn" (1887). The initial atmospheric description, seven pages in length, begins as follows:

It was a ghostly place in broad daylight, if the glimmer that stole in through the dense forest that surrounded it when the sun was directly overhead deserved this delusive name. At any other time it was – why, we were afraid even to talk about it!! and as to venturing within its gloomy borders, it was currently believed among us that to do so was to bring upon the intruder

---

[78] Ibid., 177.
[79] Ibid., 43.

certain death. I knew every foot of the ground, wet and dry, within five miles of my father's house, except this plantation,... but the swamp and "ma'shes" that surrounded this place I had never invaded. The boldest hunter on the plantation would call off his dogs and go home if they struck a trail that crossed the soggy boundary line of "No Haid Pawn".[80]

Even the runaway slaves who occasionally left their homes and took to the swamps and woods, impelled by the cruelty of their overseers, or by a desire for a vain counterfeit of freedom, never tried this swamp, but preferred to be caught and returned home to invading its awful shades.[81]

A number of terrible and bloody legends are related about the plantation, and these flow through the narrator's memory while he sits in the old house taking refuge from a nocturnal rainstorm:

My surroundings were too vivid to my apprehension. The awful traditions of the place, do what I might to vanquish them, would come to mind. The original building of the house and its blood-stained foundation stones; the dead who had died of the pestilence that had raged afterwards; the bodies carted by scores and buried in the soggy earth of the graveyard, whose trees loomed up through the broken window; the dreadful story of the dead paddling about the swamp in their coffins; and, above all, the gigantic maniac whose ferocity even murder could not satiate, and who had added to murder awful mutilation.... It all passed through my mind as I sat there in the darkness, and no effort of my will could keep my thoughts from dwelling on it. The terrific thunder, out crashing a thousand batteries, at times engrossed my attention; but it always reverted to that scene of horror; and if I dozed, the slamming of the loose blinds, or the terrific fury of the storm, would suddenly startle me.[82]

Aside from the haunted-house motif, Page occasionally shows characters responding aesthetically to a scene, but this device is found in a developed stage only in stories laid outside of the author's native region. The narrator in "Elsket" is eloquent about the beauties of the mountains in Norway; in "Miss Godwin's Inheritance" (1907), he lingers upon the beauties of the flower-garden slopes on the coast of Maine; in "A Brother to Diogenes" (1907), he is overcome by the magnificence of the Rockies in the Far West. In the last of these stories, which may be taken as a fair example, the old philosopher speaks in this fashion:

---

[80] *In Ole Virginia*, 162.
[81] Ibid., 164.
[82] Ibid., 181-82.

So I went over most of the Rockies and Sierras, but, little by little, as I wandered up and down, I began to feel how good it was to be up there, even if I didn't strike gold, but just found the air clear and clean, as dew, and the earth quiet and undisturbed and carpeted with flowers, with the creatures God made.[83]

I have my art galleries, too, with such pictures as no artist but one ever painted, and they are all taken care of for me. The colors are from Him who made the heavens blue and stained these hills green, who paints the sunrise and sunset and spangled the sky with stars.[84]

Whenever Page's foreign characters show signs of aesthetic sensitivity to their surroundings, they generally prefer the natural scene to the cultivated, as the preceding quotations illustrate. Even more apt is old Miss Abby's comment upon her neighbour's improvements in "Leander's Light" (1907); "'Pears to me," she says, "like they were takin' one of God's landscapes and makin' a painted picture of it. But it's none of *my* business. I suppose he's trying to forge something up there."[85] Page's own aesthetic interest in landscape grew rapidly during his last years of authorship, after he had exhausted his Virginia plantation materials and had spent a great deal of his time away from home. But as for artistic merit, he may as well have ceased his efforts as a writer of short stories with *Bred in the Bone* in 1904.

In all of Allen's principal short stories the setting stands in close relation to character. Viewing man as a part of nature, the author could not find it consistent with his theory to completely separate the two. If for literary purposes he found it necessary to follow the tradition of choosing particular people and temporarily lifting them out of their element for description and analysis, he did not wish to forget the factors which had determined their development. Consequently he brought nature into the picture in various ways as a means of making intelligible his portrayal of individual people. Because the older writers had been prone to extol the special virtues of man and to demean the other forms of life, Allen would stress the basic nature of man and expose the folly of such discrimination. This objective, however, only gradually arose in his mind. It had

[83] *Under the Crust* (New York, 1907), 123-124.
[84] Ibid., 133.
[85] Ibid., 188.

its beginning in "Two Gentlemen of Kentucky" and "The White Cowl" in 1888 and rose to a full expression in "Summer in Arcady" (1896). In the earlier stories Nature seems to have been in Allen's mind as being equal to man and cooperating with him in his pursuit of his own ends. Sometimes there was a deep sense of companionship between the two. But eventually Nature became an equivalent to Fate, a tremendous intelligent Force with a single purpose to fullfill throughout all forms of life. In "Summer in Arcady" a young Kentucky swain has no more notion of the true explanations of his conduct than a summer butterfly. Allen's conceptions of nature as a personality will be reserved for the next chapter; for the present only his use of a passive nature in close relation to humanity is being considered.

One theme which Allen particularly liked was the maladjustment of human beings to their physical environment as a result either of failing to meet changing conditions or, more frequently, of possessing a disposition which must rebel against the restrictions of unnatural, though sacred, institutions. "Two Gentlemen of Kentucky" (*Century*, 1888) is a tragic story of a fixed character in a changing environment. It is to be associated with Allen's article entitled "Uncle Tom at Home" (*Century*, 1887), "a description of the same background with a good deal of actuality behind it".[86] Though the old Southern gentleman is admittedly a type character, his natural surroundings are authentic and unique. "Those grounds", the author remarks – "were there ever any others like them – lawns, hedges, forest trees and evergreens, vines, fruits, flowers, birds, sun and shade, songs and quiet! They are all a mirage now lifted away from the earth."[87] Allen's method in the story is to describe the scene chiefly in the earlier part and then to portray in the remaining portion its human "landmarks", Colonel Fields and his black servant, Peter. To quote from "Two Gentlemen of Kentucky",

The reader will have a clearer insight into the character and past career of Colonel Romulus Fields by remembering that he represented a fair type of

[86] "Introductory Sketch", *Flute and Violin and Other Kentucky Tales and Romances* (New York, 1908), x.
[87] Ibid., xi.

that social order which had existed in rank perfection over the blue-grass plains of Kentucky during the final decades of the old regime. Perhaps of all agriculturists in the United States the inhabitants of that region had spent the most nearly idyllic life, on account of the beauty of the climate, the richness of the land, the spacious comfort of their homes, the efficiency of their negroes, and the characteristic contentedness of their dispositions. Thus nature and history combined to make them a peculiar class, a cross between the aristocratic and the bucolic, being as simple as shepherds and as proud as kings.[88]

So many sad memories assault the Colonel while he continues his idle life on the old homestead that he flees with Peter to Lexington to begin a new life of friendships and activity. Failing pathetically at this, he withdraws again to remain in isolation until his death. Only the trees and flowers and Peter remain unchanged to comfort him during his last days. He finds peace only in his garden, touching his favorite China pinks "softly with his fingers, as though they were the fragrant, never-changing symbols of voiceless communication with the past".[89] In this story Nature is a refuge for the old gentleman, for in a Kentucky garden she is herself "folded in the calm of Eternal Peace".[90]

"The White Cowl" (*Century*, 1888) has also a unique setting and type characters, and is to be associated with the author's article entitled "A Home of the Silent Brotherhood". This story, as well as the article, Knight tells us, "was the outcome of Allen's visit to the most picturesque spot in Kentucky, the abbey of La Trappe at Gethsemane, near Bardstown".[91] Young Father Paleman, though reared in the most artificial and restricted environment conceivable, is nevertheless a full-blooded man. After giving an atmospheric picture of the abbey, Allen presents the young monk in a magnificent garden, where "he drank in eagerly all the sweet influences of the perfect day".[92] Gradually the scene of natural perfection around him begins to stir up within him a kindred sense of ecstasy and strange longing. This effect was only "natural", for

[88] Ibid., 101.
[89] Ibid., 125.
[90] Ibid., 97.
[91] Knight, op cit., 71.
[92] *Flute and Violin*, 138.

Father Paleman was himself a part of the pure and the beautiful nature around him. His heart was like some great secluded crimson flower that is ready to burst open in a passionate seeking of the sun. As he sat thus in the midst of Nature's joyousness and irresponsible unfoldings, and peaceful consummations, he forgot hunger and thirst and weariness in a feeling of delicious languor. But beneath even this, and more subtle still, was the stir of restlessness and the low fever of vague desire for something wholly beyond his experience.[93]

In this story Nature is beginning to show its unconquerable power. Paleman cannot be happy within the monastery because nature did not fit him for monkish life, and "nature is never thwarted without suffering".[94] Religious faith, the author wishes to show, is wrong if it warms only "by extinguishing the fires of nature".[95] A single encounter with an attractive woman is enough to undo all the effects of his teaching and to cause his fundamental nature to assert itself. The central theme of this story is not the conflict of love and duty, as Knight believes,[96] but the folly and wastefulness of subverting the purposes of nature.

A companion story, "Sister Dolorosa" (*Century*, 1890), is not to be credited with actuality, for the author tells us that it

was framed and the material for it gotten long before I ever visited the convent; and it would have been written had I never gone thither. What my visit to the convent actually gave me was local color, and this I could have gotten merely by walking across the fields in that region and by looking at the convent buildings half a mile away.[97]

"Sister Dolorosa" is essentially the same story as "A White Cowl" with a young nun in a convent substituted for the monk of La Trappe Abbey. Like Father Paleman, this young woman is an excellent specimen of humanity. "Love and sympathy are the strongest principles of her nature", and her womanhood is only poorly concealed by her black garments of the convent. After trying in vain to satisfy her desires through imaginary experience, she seeks a sympathetic companionship in growing plants.

[93] Ibid., 138-39.
[94] Ibid., 144.
[95] Ibid., 141.
[96] See Knight, op. cit., 77.
[97] "Certain Criticisms of Certain Tales", *Century* Magazine, LXII, 154 (May, 1891).

With inexpressible relief she turned from medieval books to living nature; and her beautiful imagination... now began to bind nature to her with fellowships which quieted the need of human association. She had long been used to feign correspondence with the fathers of the Church; she now established intimacies with dumb companions, and poured out her heart to them in confidence.[98]

The hero, Gordon Helm, is strong and healthy, an unrestrained child of nature, a hunter who spends much of his time in the forests. "The irresistible effect of his appearance was an impression of simple joyousness in life. There seemed to be stored up in him, the warmth of the sunshine of his land; the gentleness of its fields; the kindness of its landscapes."[99] Consequently the very sight of a place of confinement like a convent irritates him. Especially in the graveyard of nuns "the aspect and spirit of the place" was "the last thing needed to wring the heart of Helm with dumb pity and an ungovernable anguish of rebellion... His whole nature cried aloud against it".[100]

Another device which Allen employs to relate character to passive setting is the symbolic use of particular scenes for purposes of exemplification. By this method nice, emotionally shaded meanings are conveyed, either to the characters or directly to the reader. In the earlier stories this device was used only incidentally, but it grew upon Allen, along with his interest in nature, until it became a regular part of his narrative technique, and entire stories became allegories or parables.

In one of the earlier stories, "Two Gentlemen from Kentucky", this example occurs, hardly more than a figure of speech:

After a long, dry summer you may have seen two gnarled old apple-trees, that stood with interlocked arms on the western slope of some quiet hillside, make a melancholy show of blooming out again in the autumn of the year and dallying with the idle buds that mock their sapless branches. Much the same was the belated, fruitless efflorescence of the Colonel and Peter.[101]

[98] *Flute and Violin*, 193.
[99] Ibid., 198.
[100] Ibid., 217.
[101] Ibid., 109.

In "Sister Dolorosa" the author briefly interprets the nun's whole nature in terms of landscape; he sees her as

some long, sloping mountain-side, with an upper zone of ever-lingering snow for childhood, below this a green vernal belt for maidenhood, and near the foot fierce summer heats and summer storms for womanhood.[102]

For Helm the distant view of the convent walls signifies the "remaining barriers between them".[103] "He would brush aside the mere cobwebs that separate him from his lover", but he cannot see, with the reader, that over the convent church, "from the zenith of the sky down to the horizon there rested on outstretched wings, rank above rank and pinion brushing pinion, a host of white, angelic cloudshapes, as though guarding the sacred portal".[104] Later in the night, however, after Helm has secretly stolen his way into the sacred sanctuary,

the host of seraphic cloud-forms had fled across the sky; and as she turned her eyes upward to the heavens, there looked down upon her from their severe, untroubled heights only the stars, that never henceforth should she look upon them without being reminded of how her own will had wandered from its orbit. The moon rained its steady beams upon the symbol of the sacred heart on her bosom, until it seemed to throb with the agony of the crucifixion.[105]

The symbolic use of nature in "Summer in Arcady" (1894) is somewhat more pronounced. The flight of butterflies suggests to Allen a universal pattern:

How they ride the blue billows of air, circling, pursuing, mounting higher and higher, the first above the second, the second above the first; then whirling downward again, and so ever fleeing and seeking, floating and clinging, blindly, helplessly, under the transport of all-compelling, unfathomable Nature!....

Can you consider a field of butterflies and not think of the blindly wandering, blindly loving, quickly passing human race? Can you observe two young people at play on the meadows of Life and Love without seeing in them a pair of these brief moths of the sun?[106]

[102] Ibid., 219.
[103] Ibid., 239.
[104] Ibid., 240-41.
[105] Ibid., 244-45.
[106] *Summer in Arcady* (New York, 1902), 3-4.

The central idea of the story, as stated in these passages, is that the correspondence between human and animal life is due to the common origin of their impulses. This parallelism is often reiterated, as in this reflective comment upon Hilary and his dog:

They were close to Nature as they lay there that summer night – those two young animals. The dog was better trained, and had behind him generations of better trained fathers.[107]

Or in this comparison of Daphne and the butterfly:

Nature at that moment made no difference between the insect and the girl in her instructions. She said to the butterfly: "Enter this woods. You may find what you seek – rest from your restlessness, happiness, companionship".[108]

Allen's novelette, "The Bride of the Mistletoe" (1909), is built up around the symbolism in a Christmas tree and harks back to ancient pagan tree-worship: druidism and pantheism. A wife sees a limb of a tree embrace her husband's shoulder and she understands that he is Nature's own and henceforth lost to her.

As she followed behind, the old mystery of the woods seemed at last to have taken bodily possession of him. The fir was riding on his shoulder, its arms met fondly around his neck, its fingers were carressing his hair. And it whispered back jeeringly to her through the twilight:
"Say farewell to him! He was once yours; he is yours no longer. He dandles the child of the forest over his shoulder instead of his children by you in the house. He belongs to Nature; and as Nature calls he will always follow – though it should lead him over the precipice or into the flood."[109]

The symbolism in Allen's later stories, as this and the preceding selection indicate, is usually found in conjunction with personifications, which will be treated in the next chapter.

Sarah Orne Jewett, during the first decade of her New England stories, from about 1875 to 1885, was just beginning to think, in sociological and cultural terms, of man's relation to his environment. Beginning with *A White Heron and Other Stories* (1886), her work reveals an intellectual awareness of the shaping forces and powers which had

[107] Ibid., 76.
[108] Ibid., 108.
[109] *A Bride of the Mistletoe*, 63.

produced the New England social structure which, in her Deephaven days, she had known only from memory and through her childhood emotions. But "The White Heron" was not the first evidence of her intellectual awakening that was later to mature her style. In "Lady Ferry" (1879), an early story already mentioned, the young writer makes this observation:

One often hears of the influence of climate upon character; there is a strong influence of place; and the inanimate things which surround us indoors and out make us follow out in our lives their own silent characteristics. We unconsciously catch the tone of every house in which we live, and of every view of the outward, material world which grows familiar to us, and we are influenced by surroundings nearer and closer still than the climate or the country which we inhabit.[110]

In her early essay entitled "River Driftwood", in the *Atlantic* for October, 1881, however, she was willing to limit the extent to which outside influences determine one's character. She says:

The shape of its [a river's] shores and the quality of the soil it passes over determine certain things about it, but the life of it is something by itself, as the life of a man is separate from the circumstances in which he is placed.... I should like to know the beginning and headwater of my river.[111]

At the same time she was reflecting about the universality of natural laws that extend throughout the world, indiscriminate and objective in their operations. In "An October Ride", in *Country By-Ways* (1881), she pauses to reflect:

The relationship of untamed nature to what is tamed and cultivated is a very curious and subtle thing to me; I do not know if every one feels it so intensely. In the darkness of an early autumn evening I sometimes find myself whistling a queer tune that chimes in with the crickets' piping and the cries of the little creatures around me in the garden. I have no thought of the rest of the world. I wonder what I am; there is a strange self-consciousness, but I am only part of one great existence which is called nature. The life in me is a bit of all life, and where I am happiest is where I find that which is next of kin to me in friends, or trees, or hills, or seas, or beside a flower, when I turn back more than once to look into its face.
The world goes on year after year. We can use its forces, and shape and

---

[110] *Old Friends and New*, 188.
[111] *Country By-Ways*, 2.

HUNT LIBRARY
CARNEGIE-MELLON UNIVERSITY

mould them, and perfect this thing or that, but we cannot make new forces; we can use only the tools we find to carve the wood we find.[112]

This notion of the equality of man and the lower forms of life from the standpoint of natural forces may be found frequently reiterated. Even in "The Queen's Twin", in the *Atlantic* for February, 1899, the narrator looks at the savage struggle of sturdy little trees on a sterile bit of soil and must

feel a sudden pity for the men and women who had been worsted after a long fight in that lonely place; one felt a sudden fear of the unconquerable, immediate forces of Nature, as in the irresistible moment of a thunderstorm.[113]

Often she has the thought that she is part of a large, orderly nature, "like an atom of quick-silver against a great mass".

These ideas do occasionally turn up in Jewett's stories, but she seldom builds a plot around the relation of character and environment. Both character and place are highly individualized in most cases, and New Englanders are thoroughly adapted to New England.[114] Unlike most local colorists, she is more likely to begin with character than place, and at first the background is often merely implied from her presentation of a character. "Miss Debby's Neighbors" (1883) begins in this way:

There is a class of elderly New England women which is fast dying out! – those good souls who have sprung from a soil full of the true New England instincts; were used to the old-fashioned ways, and whose minds were stored with quaint country lore and tradition. The fashions of the newer generations do not reach them; they are quite unconscious of the western spirit and enterprise, and belong to the old days, and to a fast-disappearing order of things.[115]

This introduction would serve as well for many of Jewett's other stories. She gives first the people, then their homes, and then the surrounding background accounting for their peculiarities. Frequently the link between character and setting that is only implied

[112] Ibid., 100-101.

[113] Sarah Orne Jewett, *The Queen's Twin and Other Stories* (Boston and New York, 1899), 16-17.

[114] Cf. Richard Cary, *Sarah Orne Jewett* (New York, 1962), 54.

[115] Sarah Orne Jewett, *The Mate of the Daylight and Friend Ashore* (Boston and New York, 1883), 190.

in the body of the story is firmly welded, poetically, figuratively, or matter-of-factly at the very end of the story. The last paragraph of "A Landless Farmer", in the *Atlantic* for May and June, 1883, runs as follows:

Heaven only knows the story of the lives that the gray old New England farmhouses have sheltered and hidden away from curious eyes as best they might. Stranger dramas than have ever been written belong to the dull-looking, quiet homes, that have seen generation after generation live and die. On the well-worn boards of these provincial theatres the great plays of life, and comedies and tragedies, with their lovers and conspirators and clowns; their Juliets and Ophelias, Shylocks and King Lears, are acted over and over and over again.[116]

In "A White Heron", the title story of the first volume of her second great decade, Jewett made a more literary use of environmental factors. Sylvia, a lonely, shy young girl of the New England forest, is torn between her love for a transient ornithologist and her loyalty to her friends in the woods, especially the white heron, which the young scientist seeks for his collection. He offers her friendship and money to relieve her poverty, but

No, she must keep silence! What is it that suddenly forbids her and makes her dumb? Has she been nine years growing and now, when the great world for the first time puts out a hand to her, must she thrust it aside for a bird's sake? The murmur of the pine's green branches is in her ears, she remembers how the white heron came flying through the golden air and how they watched the sea and the morning together, and Sylvia cannot speak; she cannot tell the heron's secret and give its life away.[117]

Most of Jewett's stories, having less plot than "The White Heron", do not clearly represent the unfolding of a character-environment problem. But in "A Neighbor's Landmark",[118] in the *Century* for September, 1893, the same theme is worked out with considerable suspense. John Packer's loyalty to his two old pines and the tradition surrounding them is effectively dramatized, but since the trees function as characters, this story belongs in a different category.

---

[116] Ibid., 53.
[117] *A White Heron and Other Stories*, 21.
[118] Included in Sarah Orne Jewett, *The Life of Nancy* (Boston and New York, 1896).

"The King of Folly Island", in *Harper's* for December, 1886, is the story of a young lady doomed by her father's obsession to pass her youth on a dismal, deserted island off the Maine coast. Her struggle to satisfy the aesthetic needs of her life in this desolation seems pathetic and wasteful to Frankfort, a visitor from the outside world. Nothing actually happens in the story; there is no dramatic situation. A kind of serenity surrounds Phoebe's calm submission to spiritual starvation. The qualities of the island, to which the "King" and his daughter are practically oblivious, are so unique as to impress the visitor, who possessed a "sincere interest in such individualized existence".[119] The strange sounds of the wind in the trees and the waves on the shore produce in him "a loneliness, a remoteness, a feeling of being an infinitesimal point in such a great expanse of sea and stormy sky, that was almost too heavy to be borne".[120]

In "Fair Day" (1888) may be seen an example of the thorough adaptation of a New Englander to his home environment. For Mother Bascom "There was a sense of companionship in the very weather", and "the comfortable feeling of relationship to her surroundings all served to put... [her] into a most peaceful state".[121] This same attitude is expressed by Mrs. Peet in "Going to Shrewsbury" (1889) as she is forced to leave her old homestead: "I tell ye, dear, it's hard to go an' live twenty-two miles from where you've always had your home and friends. It may divert me, but it won't be home. You might as well set out one o' my old apple-trees on the beach, so't could see the waves come in, – there wouldn't be no please to it."[122]

"By the Morning Boat" (1890) is exceptional in beginning with descriptive setting, but the initial description proves to be important as a preparation for a character's departure from his old home environment. The small gray house on the lonely coast of Maine, "where balsam firs and bay berry bushes send forth their fragrance

---

[119] Sarah Orne Jewett, *The King of Folly Island and Other People* (Boston and New York, 1888), 19.
[120] Ibid., 26-27.
[121] *Strangers and Wayfarers*, 131.
[122] Ibid., 141.

far seaward,... and the tide runs splashing in and out among the weedy ledges",[123] recurs at the very end of the story, seen through the loving eyes of young Elisha as he takes the morning boat to seek his fortunes in a more prosperous country:

The whole landscape faded from his eyes except that far-away gray house; his heart leaped back with love and longing; he gazed and gazed, until a height of green forest came between and shut the picture out. Then the country boy went on alone to make his way in the wide world.[124]

In "Along Shore", in *The Country of the Pointed Firs*, the narrator or rather expositor, notices in the outdoor New Englander's appearance a definite effect of his long preoccupation with the affairs of nature. "I often wondered a great deal about the inner life and thought of these self-contained old fishermen", she confesses; "their minds seemed to be fixed upon nature and the elements rather than upon any contrivances of man." There was also a purely physical adjustment; life at sea had "affected the old fishermen's hard complexions, until one fancied that when death claimed them it could only be with the aid, not of any slender modern dart, but the good serviceable harpoon of a seventeenth century woodcut".[125]

Many such fleeting observations of the close relation of people to their surroundings are to be found in Jewett's stories. *Deephaven* and *The Country of the Pointed Firs* also reveal influences of the isolated New England scenes upon the visitor. As her biographer Matthiessen has observed, "she found herself equipped at the start of her career with... an almost complete knowledge of her environment".[126] In her old age she advised Willa Cather, "I want you to be surer of your backgrounds";[127] and this younger disciple, when she wrote many years later the preface to a selected edition of her friend's stories, included this statement:

Miss Jewett wrote of the people who grew out of the soil and the life of the country near her heart, not about exceptional individuals at war with their

[123] Ibid., 197.
[124] Ibid., 219.
[125] Sarah Orne Jewett, *The Country of the Pointed Firs*, in *The Best Stories of Sarah Orne Jewett*, 2 vols. (Boston and New York, 1925), I, 188.
[126] *Sarah Orne Jewett*, 51.
[127] *Letters*, 248.

environment. This was not a creed with her but an instinctive preference. She once laughingly told me that her head was full of dear old houses and dear old women, and that when an old house and an old woman came together in her brain with a click, she knew that a story was under way.[128]

Like Cable, Freeman saw her special region as a unique social machine, but she conceived of this machine as having run down. Says Matthiessen, she deals with a "pattern of existence" which "has been warped and twisted" as a result of the hard struggles of preceding generations.[129] In her treatment of individuals frustrated by this obsolete pattern, her work shows kinship with late nineteenth-century naturalists, despite her avowed desire to avoid them. Though in her early period she seemed aware of the shaping force of environment, particularly its power to thwart human desires, she became in later years more interested in the spiritual influences of growing things and inanimate nature upon man. "Who shall determine the limit at which the intimate connection and reciprocal influences of all forms of visible creation upon one another may stop?" she asks in "The Great Pine".[130] In a descriptive article on New England she makes the point that the early natives probably were too busy to respond aesthetically or spiritually to their surroundings, but that they nevertheless sensed some feeling toward them, if only fear or gratulation.[131]

Though Freeman does not usually devote much space to incidental scenery in her early stories, she is careful to bring out the immediate surroundings necessary to the action. There is sometimes recognition of a dominating influence of nature upon the characters. In "A Gatherer of Simples" (1887) appears a definite influence of the nature school. Aurelia Flower, like Jewett's Mrs. Todd, is a remarkable naturalist.

She loved her work, and the greenwood things were to her as friends, and the healing qualities of sarsaparilla and thoroughwort, and the sweetness of thyme and lavender, seemed to have entered into her nature, till she could almost talk with them in that way.[132]

[128] *The Best Stories of Sarah Orne Jewett*, xvi.
[129] Matthiessen, "New England Stories", 405.
[130] Mary E. Wilkins Freeman, *Six Trees* (New York, 1903), 79-80.
[131] See Mary E. Wilkins Freeman, "New England, Mother of America", *Country Life*, XXII, 27 (July 1, 1912).
[132] *A Humble Romance*, 288.

Analogies between plants and people occasionally appear, as in "An Unwilling Guest" (1887), in which Susan remarks:

I've been lookin' at that grass out there. I feel as if I'd stayed in this house so long that I'm rooted, just as the grass is in the yard. An' now they're goin' to take me up root an' all, and I'm only a poor old worn-out woman, an' I can't stan' it; I – can't – stan' it![133]

The most original feature of Freeman's use of setting in relation to character consists in her symbolism concerning man and nature. "Her chief use of setting", Pattee believes, "is Hawthornesque – the use of it symbolically, poetically, as an interpreting or contrasting touch in her human tragedy or comedy."[134] Though the results of this study favor regarding this use as secondary to her use of setting for background and ornament, it is indeed important and stands as a vital part of her narrative technique. "I want more symbolism, more mysticism", she once said; "I left that out because it struck me people did not want it, and I was forced to consider selling qualities."[135]

Though she does not let her ambition carry her as far as she might in this direction, a good deal of nature symbolism is to be found even in her early period. Many of her early stories bear the names of New England flowers in their titles and carry out a faint parallelism. "Brakes and White Vi'lets" (1887), "Cinnamon Roses" (1887), "Calla-Lilies and Hannah" (1891), and "The Scent of the Roses" (1891) are good examples. In the first of these old Mrs. Patter is "torn betwixt two loves and two longings: one for her dear Levina, and one for her dear home, with its setting of green brakes and white violets";[136] her final resolution is to "dig up a root of white vi'lets an' some brakes, so – I kin take 'em with me".[137] In the second story of this group, "Cinnamon Roses", the key flower symbolizes the affection of an old maid for the little cottage which she once shared with a beautiful and popular sister. The house was inaccessible because of the luxurious

---

[133] Ibid., 339.
[134] Pattee, *Side-Lights on American Literature*, 201-202.
[135] See Ibid., 195.
[136] *A Humble Romance*, 113.
[137] Ibid., 117.

growth of cinnamon roses. The intention of a later owner of the property to destroy them, and Elsie's curious means of stopping him, makes up the main situation. "Calla-Lillies and Hannah" opens with a discussion of the peculiar characteristics of the fickle plant which will bloom for some people and not for others.[138] Though Hannah has been accused of theft and turned out of the church, the implication is that she is nevertheless innocent because her calla-lillies, which she herself strangely resembles, bloom magnificently. "The Scent of the Roses" is constructed with a rather complex symbolism around the flower concerned, and every possible effort is made to keep the suggestion of roses prominently in the reader's imagination. The main characters, two sisters, are both roses, one of them fresh and the other somewhat faded. The house is constantly filled with the odor of roses, for Clarissa's chief occupation is to preserve the blossoms of this plant, as a former lover had once recommended. Spring brings fresh roses, Clarissa's lover unexpectedly returns to her, and young Anne at the last carries on with the rose-gathering tradition.

Objects other than flowers appear as the focal center for symbolism in other early stories by Mrs. Freeman, but essentially the same procedure is followed. A quite different kind of symbolism, however, and one which makes use of outdoor scenes and landscapes, appears in some of the stories. In "An Honest Soul" (1887), included in her first volume, a strong contrast is built up between the dismal indoor life of old Martha Patch and the bright green spot outside her house. In "The Bar Light-House" (1887) a man and his wife find totally different symbolical meanings in the same landscape:

Jackson Reed simply looked out on nature and into his own soul, and took in as plain incontrovertible facts the broken bridge, the tossing sea, his little wind-swept, sandstrewn garden-patch, and God in heaven. Neither proved the other or nullified the other; they were simply *there*. But Sarah Reed, looking out on the frail, unsafe bridge... and the mighty, senseless sea which had swallowed up her father and a brother whom she had idolized, and the poor little tender green things trying to live under her window,

---

[138] *A New England Nun*, 100.

had seen in them so many denials of either God's love and mercy, or his existence.[139]

More frequently there is an apparently coincidental agreement or contrast in mood between a character and the surrounding landscape, as in this example from "Old Lady Pingree":

There was a beautiful clear sunset that night... All her heart was full of a sweet, almost rapturous peace. She had had a bare, hard life; and now the one earthly ambition, pitiful and melancholy as it seemed, which had kept its living fire was gratified.[140]

At the conclusion of "A New England Nun" (1891), Louisa is happy because she has just escaped a marriage which would have ended her serene and placid way of living; and the atmosphere around her, at that moment, is "filled with the sounds of the busy harvest of men and birds and bees" and "sweet calls... and long hummings".[141] "A Poetess" (1891) ends with the death of Miss Dole, who is gladdened, at the very last, by the minister's promise to celebrate her in a poem.

She smiled, and the sweetness of the smile was as evident through the drawn lines of her mouth as the old red in the leaves of a withered rose. The sun was setting; a red beam flashed softly over the top of the hedge and lay along the opposite wall; then the bird in the cage began to chirp. He chirped faster and faster until he thrilled into a triumphant song.[142]

"A Discovered Pearl" (1891) also concludes with a harmony of pleasant landscape and happiness in the part of a character:

It was sunset when she went home the last time. It had stopped snowing and there was a clear, yellow sky in the west. A flock of sparrows flew whistling around one of the maples.... Lucy Glynn sped along. Whether wisely or not, she was full of all Christmas joy. She had given at last her Christmas gift, which she had been treasuring for twenty years.[143]

At the end of "The Revolt of Mother" the happy reconciliation of Adoniram and Sarah Penn is echoed by a tranquil landscape:

After the supper dishes were cleared away and the milk-pans washed,

---

[139] *A Humble Romance*, 181-82.
[140] Ibid., 162.
[141] *A New England Nun*, 17.
[142] Ibid., 159.
[143] Ibid., 267.

Sarah went out to him. The twilight was deepening. There was a clear green glow in the sky. Before them stretched the smooth level of the field; in the distance was a cluster of haystacks like the huts of a village; the air was very cool and calm and sweet. The landscape might have been an ideal one of peace.[144]

In these stories the final emotional key set by the dramatic situation is prolonged by the tone of the scenic image that is used to harmonize with it. Some of Freeman's strongest story endings are of this type.

In her later period, Freeman, in dealing with man's relation to his environment, swings away from her former theses of frustration and interests herself more and more in man's life in relation to plants and animals. As in the earlier stories, the two chief ways in which she reveals this relationship are by symbolism or parallelism on one hand, and by showing nature's influences upon people on the other.

Her symbolism and parallelism in this period are even more rife than in the earlier stories. *Understudies* (1901) is a series of parallels between nature's little creatures, especially small animals, and the people whom their lives happen to touch. In "The Squirrel", to choose one example, a pair of squirrels is shown to be very much like the man and his wife whose walnuts have been stolen, for

The same delight in their providence, and sense of self gratulation, and security as to the future, were over them as over the old couple in the farm-house. They too looked forward to peace and comfort on earth; as for the unknown future, they did not dream it existed. They had no religious hope, but their utter lack of questioning made them too trustful for any anxiety.[145]

In "The Butterfly" (1904), in a later volume, Mr. Brown uses "a gorgeous black-and-gold butterfly" as a symbol of the good element in his unfaithful wife's character:

"I've about come to the conclusion that there's always a butterfly, or something that's got wings, that comes from everything, and if you look

144 Ibid., 468.
145 *Understudies*, 43.

sharp you'll see it, and there can't anything hinder your havin' that, anyhow, and – maybe that's worth more than all the rest."[146]

At the end of the story he stands "staring absently out of the window at the flooding of the rain which was washing off some of the dust of the world".[147] Typical of Freeman's manner in her last collection, *Edgewater People* (1918), are such remarks as "People as well as flowers escape from gardens, and legitimate environments... No particular stigma attaches to them for so doing";[148] and "It may be that people, like landscapes, have their color-schemes."[149]

Mrs. Freeman's use of nature as an influence upon character in the later stories can be more adequately illustrated. Like the nun in Allen's "Sister Dolorosa", the sentimental spinster in "Evelina's Garden" (1898) finds in her love for flowers an outlet for her suppressed emotions:

The roses and pinks, the poppies and the heart's-ease, were to this maiden-woman, who had innocently and helplessly outgrown her maiden heart, in the place of all the loves of life which she had missed. Her affections had forced an outlet in roses; they exhaled sweetness in pinks, and twined and clung in honeysuckle-vines. The daffodils, when they came up in the spring, comforted her like the smiles of children; when she saw the first rose, her heart leaped as at the face of a lover.[150]

In "Silence" (1898) old Woman Goody Crane, who has been suspected of witchcraft, tells David his sweetheart's mental aberration can be cured by the mystic powers of the full moon. True to her prediction, the lover is restored to her senses in the beautiful valley which "lay in the moonlight like a landscape of silver".[151] In "Mountain-Laurel" (1901) the hero derives a strong aesthetic and imaginative stimulus from the laurel bush:

Sitting there beneath the shade of his splendid symbolic flowers,... he was one of the happiest crowned heads in the world.[152]

---

146 Mary E. Wilkins Freeman, *The Givers* (New York, 1904), 261.
147 Ibid., 265.
148 Mary E. Wilkins Freeman, *Edgewater People* (New York, 1918), 101.
149 Ibid., 261.
150 *Silence and Other Stories*, 124.
151 Ibid., 54.
152 *Understudies*, 189-90.

The short stories included in *Six Trees* (1903), a companion volume to *Understudies*, make use of subtle connections and influences between particular trees and particular people. Sam Maddox and his wife lived in such miserable quarters that one could scarcely bear to visit them; yet there grew in their yard an apple tree so magnificent that the very sight of it in full bloom "would vanquish squalor and the despair of humanity".[153] Living beside this tree, they came under its strong influence:

The splendid apple-tree bloomed and sweetened, and the man and woman, in a certain sense, tasted and drank it until it became a part of themselves, and there was, in the midst of the poverty and shiftlessness of the Maddox yard a great inflorescence of beauty for its redemption.[154]

In "Joy", included in *The Givers* (1904), William is one who lives close to nature. "The little front yard was gay with flowers every summer, and his very soul seemed to leap to new reaches of life and color to keep pace with the blossoms."[155] In "The Fair Lavinia" (1907) Harry smells the "bouquet of perfume"[156] from flowers and fruit blossoms and "the vital breath of the new grass" and realizes that there is "emanating from his own soul a fragrance which accorded well with the spring".[157] As these examples indicate, there can be little doubt that Freeman is properly classed, at least in her later period, with the nature writers of the eighteen-nineties.

Eggleston's tendency to regard human life as phenomena for the social scientist led him to produce a type of story in which characters function merely as elements in a social structure. He was conscious of the external shaping forces in his own environment and in all other parts of society; it was apparently only his religious beliefs that prevented his maintaining a mechanistic point of view.

"The Gunpowder Plot" (1871) is a story of a fanatic philosopher and nature enthusiast whose chief ambition was to "bring his daughter's mind into intimate relations with nature",[158] and

---

[153] *Six Trees*, 173.
[154] Ibid., 207.
[155] *The Givers*, 144.
[156] *The Fair Lavinia*, 9.
[157] Ibid., 10.
[158] *Duffels*, 93.

to marry her to a man who "lives in the arcana of nature and reads her secrets".[159] With this purpose he took her to a secluded frontier region. "There is no place so lonesome as a prairie", the author comments; "the horizon is so wide, and the earth is so empty."[160] The surroundings exerted an unfortunate influence upon her mind:

Cut off from human sympathy, she used to sit at the gabled window of the cabin and look out over the boundless meadow until it seemed to her that she would lose her reason. The wild geese screaming to one another overhead, the bald eagles building in the solitary elm that grew by the river, the flocks of great white pelicans that were fishing on the beach of Swan Lake, three miles away, were all objects of envy to the lonesome heart of the girl; for they had companions of their kind – were husbands and wives and parents and children, while she – here she checked her thoughts lest she should be disloyal to her father.[161]

At this point the author veers toward a pessimistic and mechanistic conception:

To her disordered fancy the universe seemed to be a wheel. The sun and the stars came up and went down over the monotonous sea of grass with a frightful regularity, and she could not tell whether there was a God or not. When she thought of God at all, it was a relentless giant turning the crank that kept the sky going round. The universe was an awful machine.... For the great hard fate that turned the prairie universe round with a crank motion had also – so it seemed to her – snatched away from her the object of her love.[162]

Thus skepticism and unhappiness are the sole fruit of all her father's teachings in Rousseau, Pestalozzi, Froebel, and Herbert Spencer. But a miracle happens to restore her faith; she finds a lover who meets both her own and her father's approval, an "uncontaminated child of Nature, the self-educated combination of civilized and savage man". The universe becomes purposive and intelligible to the girl for the first time since her mother's death. God seems to her no longer "a cruel monster turning a crank";

[159] Ibid., 105.
[160] Ibid., 93.
[161] Ibid., 94-95.
[162] Ibid., 95.

now "every star seems to be an eye through which God is looking at me, as my mother used to".[163]

"The New Cashier", from the *Century*, December, 1892, may also be considered a story of environment. Miss Wakefield, the girl from Cedar Falls, Iowa, brings her country friendliness with her to the city, where it is mistaken for offensive familiarity.

In "Priscilla" the village heroine must choose between two suitors: one is the Marquis d'Entremont, the only man her equal in culture she has ever known; the other is a colorless person, Henry Stevens, an old schoolmate. Henry and Priscilla are adapted to the same environment; they have "looked on the same green hills, known the same people, been molded of the same strong religious feeling".[164] She undoubtedly loves the Marquis more, yet realizes that marrying him would change her whole mode of life; "she must bear with a husband whose mind was ever in a state of unrest and skepticism, and she must meet the great world".[165]

One of Eggleston's most successful studies of environment is "Periwinkle", a story which reveals the artificiality of city life and the insincerity of city people in comparison with the genuineness of country life and the honesty of country folk. Henrietta Newton, a pretty and talented country girl, goes to New York to live with a silly aunt in order to study art. Her old sweetheart, Rob Riley, is awed and estranged by her new surroundings, and a reconciliation is effected only after her return to East Weston, her native country village.

"Ben: A Story for May-Day" shows several stages of a bound boy's reaction to his surroundings. At the beginning of the story he looks through the tiny gable window from his attic room in a dingy farmhouse to see, covered with fog, "a landscape associated in his mind with toil and hard treatment". Later the fog clears and

For the first time since he had lived and worked on "Pogue's Hill", Ben took in the beauty of the landscape, wondering, as he saw the rising sun shimmering on the river and gilding the windows of the village, that he

[163] Ibid., 112.
[164] Ibid., 168.
[165] Ibid., 173.

had been blind so long. And the peace of the sun and sky and river entered into his soul as he stood staring out of that gable-window.[166]

After the day has come and gone, bringing the boy a new experience but also a great deal of shame and sadness, he looks out of the window once more. Had he been in a proper mood, he might have seen that

the moon was shining on the green pastures, the low-murmuring brook ("branch" they call it in the "dialect") looked like a thread of silver, the trees on the hill were asleep, and even the long tresses of the weeping willow among the ghost-like gravestones were not swayed by a breath; and the bosom of the river lay all white and pure and peaceful in the light.[167]

But the young boy is "chafing under his limitations, stimulated by his passions": therefore

The great deep picture framed by the little gable-window was full of troublous tokens. The brook was fretting at the stones, the willows were bemoaning the sorrow of the world, the dark maples were threatening giants against the sky, and the "ghostly sycamores" by the river's brink were palisades to shut him in.[168]

Nowhere else in all of his fiction did Eggleston show so much affinity with the conventionalized local colorists as in this exceptional story.

Garland, in his tendency toward naturalism, may be associated with Freeman, though he stands much closer to Dreiser and Norris. Garland is mechanistic in his portrayal of defeated and victimized mankind; he is also deterministic – and almost positivistic – in his philosophical conception. To quote Van Doren,

His men wrestle fearfully with sand and mud and drought and blizzard, goaded with mortgages which may at almost any moment snatch away all that labor and parsimony have stored up. His women, endowed with no matter what initial hopes and charms, are sacrificed to overwork and deprivations, and drag out maturity and old age on the weariest treadmill. The pressure of life simply is too heavy to be borne except by the ruthless and crafty. Mr. Garland, though nourished on the popular legend of the frontier, had come to feel that the "song of emigration had been, in effect, the hymn of fugitives." Illusion no less than reality had tempted Americans

---

[166] "Ben: A Story for May-Day", 71.
[167] Ibid., 74.
[168] Ibid., 75.

toward their far frontiers, and the enormous mass, once under way, had rolled stubbornly westward, crushing all its members who might desire to hesitate or reflect.[169]

So long as the frontier was open, pioneering was inevitable;[170] with its closing, the defeat of the Western farmer, unless he was an unscrupulous cheat, was also inevitable.[171]

In "A Branch Road", the opening story in *Main-Travelled Roads*, a victimized farm wife of thirty is rescued by a girlhood lover from her wretched murderous life. After her release, however, no amount of subsequent happiness can repay her for the youth and beauty that are lost to her forever. In "Up the Coolly", Garland's thesis is still more evident. By representing two brothers of about equal endowments, one having spent his life in the East, the other having clung to the farm, Garland shows the deadening effects of the Western farm environment. "A man like me is helpless," says Grant, worn to such callousness of spirit as to make reparation impossible. "Just like a fly in a pan of molasses. There's no escape for him. The more he tears around, the more liable he is to rip his legs off."[172] Howard, the successful brother, realizes for the first time the real secret of his superior fortune. "Circumstances made me and crushed you. That's all there is about that. Luck made me and cheated you. It ain't right."[173]

"Among the Corn Rows" is a story of a Norwegian farm girl's runaway marriage with a man whom she does not love, but whose unexpected proposal she accepts merely because of her oppression at home. "The Return of a Private" portrays a common soldier who returns from four years of military sevice in the South to take up his hard, monotonous life with his family on a little mortgaged farm. He has nothing to look forward to but poverty and endless toil. In "Under the Lion's Paw" a farmer is cheated out of the fruits of three years' drudgery by a landlord who makes him pay for his own improvements on the farm he has an option to purchase.

---

[169] Van Doren, *Contemporary American Novelists*, 41.
[170] See "Drifting Crane" in *Prairie Folks*, 139-48.
[171] See "Lucretia Burns" in *Other Main-Travelled Roads*, especially 103-104.
[172] *Main-Travelled Roads*, 113.
[173] Ibid., 127.

Hazard points out the fact that "Hoskins' lack of foresight is not the cause of his misfortune. He would have been powerless to help himself in any event; without capital, he had to take land at Butler's terms or go without. It is not Hoskins' simplicity but the disappearance of the frontier that makes possible Butler's demand for the unearned increment."[174]

"The Creamery Man" reflects the absurdity of the social system in the farming section based upon land property and having no relation to real accomplishment or character. In "A Day's Pleasure" a farm woman seeks despairingly for a little bit of color and aesthetic enjoyment in the small town near her home. It is by the merest accident that she finds a friend; under ordinary circumstances her efforts to find any sort of pleasure would have been useless. "Mrs. Ripley's Trip" is the pathetic study of an old woman who finally realizes her ambition to take a trip East to see her relatives after having "stuck right to the stove an' churn without a day or a night off" for twenty-three years.[175] "God's Ravens" is an indictment of village life, showing the difficulty of an intelligent man in adapting himself to its narrow, uncharitable ways.

In *Other Main-Travelled Roads* (1910) the naturalistic type of story continues in the majority. In "William Bacon's Man" the theme of an artificial class distinction is resumed. "Elder Pill, Preacher" and "A Day of Grace" are intimate, disgusting pictures of the efforts of crude frontier evangelism upon the more credulous farming people. "Lucretia Burns", the strongest story in this collection, brings out more clearly than anywhere else Garland's thesis concerning "the ugliness, the monotony, the bestiality, the hopelessness of life on the farm".[176] Lucretia blames her husband for the misery that surrounds her, and, indeed, the evil disposition which he reveals to her would warrant her hatred for him. But Douglas Radbourn, an educated outsider, can easily see that even Burns' gross nature is a result of the conditions under which he is forced to live:

---

[174] Hazard, *Frontier in American Fiction*, 266.
[175] *Main-Travelled Roads*, 265.
[176] Hazard, op. cit., 265.

"You must remember that such toil brutalizes a man; it makes him callous, selfish, unfeeling, necessarily. A fine nature must either adapt himself to its hard surroundings or die. Men who toil terribly in filthy garments day after day and year after year cannot easily keep gentle; the frost and the grime, the heat and cold, will sooner or later enter their souls. The case is not all in favor of the suffering wives and against the brutal husbands. If the farmer's wife is dulled and crazed by her routine, the farmer himself is degraded and brutalized."[177]

The dismal end of a life lived on a Western farm is depicted in "Before the Low Green Door". The bitter, overworked wife longs to die because she no longer has any hopes for the future. "We didn't expect – to work all our days", she complains. "An' the sunny place – has been always behind me, and the dark before me." So bitter has her life seemed to her that "God himself can't wipe out what has been".[178]

Among the few new stories in *Wayside Courtships* (1897), the most impressive is "The Owner of the Mill Farm", which repeats the situation in "Lucretia Burns": the estrangement of husband and wife as a result of the hard, barren lives they lead. "Drifting Crane" in *Prairie Folks* (1899) shows the Indian in conflict with the pioneer movement, which is swiftly and cruelly crushing out his life, and the hopelessness of his resistance. The more closely Garland's stories are examined, the more apt seems Howell's observation: one cannot read his fiction "without becoming more and more convinced that it is our conditioning which determines our characters, even though it does not always determine our actions".[179]

Thus far Garland's stories have been considered only with respect to the environmental clashes; now it is necessary to point out the devices wherewith his particular effects are realized. It has already been shown that Garland's desire for a significant subject matter led him to make use of Georgism, in which he was already much interested. The literary technique which Garland developed to emphasize this theme strongly resembles that employed by

[177] *Other Main-Travelled Roads*, 112-13.
[178] Ibid., 296-97.
[179] Howells, op. cit., 528.

Freeman, who, next to Garland, was the most naturalistic of the local colorists in this study.

Garland's chief device, like Freeman's, was to use his natural settings as a foil to accentuate the emotional states of the characters, whether through influences or parallelisms. But Garland's method was decidedly novel in one particular: whereas Freeman had gained her effects chiefly through drawing similarities between a character's mood and the tone of his surroundings, Garland worked chiefly through contrasts. The secret of this technique may be seen in a quotation from Millet which Garland included in his story "Up the Coolly":

I see very well the auriole of the dandelions, and the sun also, far down there behind the hills, flinging his glory upon the clouds. But not alone that – I see in the plains the smoke of the tired horses at the plough, or, on a stony hearted spot of ground, a back-broken man trying to raise himself upright for a moment to breathe. The tragedy is surrounded by glories – that is no invention of mine.[180]

In other words, a great theme is to be found in the amazing contrast, inherent in life itself, between beautiful nature and sordid man, victimized and abused, ostensibly by a social order. Garland's use of aesthetic landscapes to accent the squalor of his close-up views of human action is one of the most original and characteristic aspects of his entire literary formula. Endless examples may be cited:

They climbed slowly among the hills, and the valley they had left grew still more beautiful as the squalor of the little town was hid by the dusk of distance.[181]

The sky was magically beautiful over all this squalor and toil and bitterness, from five till seven – a moving hour. Again the falling sun streamed in broad banners across the valleys; again the blue mist lay far down the coolly over the river; the cattle called from the hills in the moistening, sonorous air; the bells came in a pleasant tangle of sound; the air pulsed with the deepening chorus of katydids and other nocturnal singers.
Sweet and deep as the very springs of his life was all this to the soul of the elder brother; but in the midst of it the younger man, in ill-smelling clothes and great boots that chafed his feet, went out to milk the cows, – on

180 *Main-Travelled Roads*, 119-20.
181 Ibid., 75.

whose legs the flies and mosquitoes swarmed, bloated with blood, – to sit by the hot side of a cow and be lashed with her tail as she tried frantically to keep the savage insects from eating her raw.[182]

The level, red light streamed through the trees, blazed along the grass, and lighted a few old-fashioned flowers into red and gold flame. It was beautiful, and Howard looked at it through his half-shut eyes as the painters do, and turned away with a sigh at the sound of blows where the wet and grimy men were assailing the frantic cows.[183]

As if a great black cloud had settled down upon him, Howard felt it all – the horror, hopelessness, imminent tragedy of it all. The glory of nature, the bounty and splendor of the sky, only made it more benumbing.[184]

In the meanwhile poor Lucretia was brooding over her life in a most dangerous fashion. All she had done and suffered from Simeon Burns came back to her till she wondered how she had endured it all. All day long in the midst of the glorious summer landscape she brooded.[185]

The wind sang in her ears; the great clouds, beautiful as heavenly ships, floated far above in the vast, dazzling deeps of blue sky; the birds rustled and chirped around her; leaping insects buzzed and clattered in the grass and in the vines and bushes. The goodness and glory of God was in the very air, the bitterness and oppression of man in every line of her face.[186]

Her faded dress settled down over her limbs, showing the swollen knees and thin calves; her hands, with distorted joints, protruding painfully from her sleeves. All about her was the ever recurring wealth and cheer of nature that knows no favor, – the bees and flies buzzing in the sun, the jay and kingbird in the poplars, the smell of strawberries, the motion of lush grass, the shimmer of corn blades tossed gayly as banners in a conquering army.[187]

Everywhere a heavenly serenity – not a footstep, not a bell, not a cry, not a crackling tree – nothing but livid light, white snow – dappled and lined with shadows, and trees etched against a starlit sky. Unutterable splendor of light and sheen and shadow. Wide wastes of snow so white the stumps stood like columns of charcoal. A night of Nature's making, when she is tired of noise and blare of color.

And in the midst of it stood the camp, with its reek of obscenity, foul odors, and tobacco smoke, to which a tortured soul must return.[188]

[182] Ibid., 102-103.
[183] Ibid., 103.
[184] Ibid., 119.
[185] *Other Main-Travelled Roads*, 91.
[186] Ibid., 95.
[187] Ibid., 114.
[188] Ibid., 288.

The preceding examples are all taken from three stories, "Up the Coolly", "Lucretia Burns", and "An Alien in the Pines". Usually Garland does not actually point out his contrasts so openly as in these examples, but they are implicit in almost all of the stories.

Second in importance among Garland's devices for linking his settings with his characters is his use of landscapes or domestic scenes as an emotional influence upon the people who observe them. Though this method is common to almost all local colorists, Garland's stories reveal a freer use of it than is to be found elsewhere except in a few short stories, such as Cable's "Jean-Ah Poquelin", Page's "No Haid Pawn", and Murfree's "Over on T'Other Mounting". Garland's device is to show his characters violently shocked or sickened by domestic scenes of squalor and misery, as the following examples indicate:

He came at last to the little farm Dingman had owned, and he stopped in sorrowful surprise.... The tears started into the man's eyes; he stood staring at it silently.[189]

A sickening chill struck into Howard's soul as he looked at it all. In the dim light he could see a figure milking a cow.[190]

The longer he stood absorbing this farm-scene, with all its sordidness, dullness, triviality, and its endless drudgeries, the lower his heart sank.[191]

Every detail of the kitchen, the heat, the flies buzzing aloft, the poor furniture, the dress of the people – all smote him like the lash of a wire whip.[192]

He woke, however, with a dull, languid pulse, and an oppressive melancholy on his heart. He looked around the little room, clean enough, but oh, how poor! how barren![193]

Beside the preceding selections should be placed several examples of the salubrious effects of natural landscapes upon the characters in Garland's stories:

Above the level belt of timber to the east a vast dome of pale undazzling gold was rising, silently and swiftly. Jays called in the thickets where the

---

189 *Main-Travelled Roads*, 44.
190 Ibid., 78.
191 Ibid., 78-79.
192 Ibid., 82.
193 Ibid., 88.

maples flamed amid the green oaks, with irregular splashes of red and orange. The grass was smooth and gray-white in color, the air was indescribably pure, resonant, and stimulating. No wonder the man sang![194]

The broadening heavens had a majesty and sweetness that made him forget the physical joy of happy youth.[195]

It [the landscape] had a certain mysterious glamour for him.[196]

The sun had set, and the coolly was getting dusk. ...He walked slowly to absorb the coolness and fragrance and color of the hour.... As he walked on, the hour and the place appealed to him with great power.[197]

As he ran lightly down the beautiful path, under oaks and hickories, past masses of poison-ivy, under hanging grapevines, through clumps of splendid hazelnut bushes loaded with great, rough, green burs, his heart threw off part of its load.[198]

The sound of the wind and the leaves moved him almost to tears.[199]

The faint clouds in the west were getting a superb flame-color above and a misty purple below, and the sun had pierced them with lances of yellow light. The air grew denser with moisture, the sounds of neighboring life began to reach the ear.... The whole scene took hold upon Seagraves with irresistible power.[200]

But the sun burst up from the plain, the prairie chickens took up their mighty chorus on the hills, robins met them on the way, flocks of wild geese, honking cheerily, drove far overhead toward the north, and, with these sounds of a golden spring day in her ears, the bride grew cheerful, and laughed.[201]

One other device in this category which appears in Garland's stories is a symbolism connecting characters with settings. It is of a relatively simple type, limited to the experiences of the characters themselves. A few instances may be quoted:

Suddenly a water-snake wriggled across the dark pool above the ford, and minnows disappeared under the shadow of the bridge. Then Will sighed, lifted his head and walked on. There seemed to be something prophetic in

[194] Ibid., 9.
[195] Idem.
[196] Ibid., 69.
[197] Ibid., 76-77.
[198] Ibid., 94-95.
[199] Ibid., 95.
[200] Ibid., 136-37.
[201] *Other Main-Travelled Roads*, 19.

it, and he drew a long breath. That's the way his plans broke and faded away.[202]

In the face of this house the seven years that he had last lived stretched away into a wild waste of time. It stood as a symbol of his wasted, ruined life.[203]

The cold and damp struck through into the alien's heart. It seemed to prophesy his dark future. He sat at his desk and looked out into the gray rain with gloomy eyes – a prisoner when he had expected to be free.[204]

The resourcefulness and inventiveness with which the local colorists tied their fictional settings into their characters is at least impressive. Though Twain and Jewett were only moderately interested in this sphere, and though Page and Eggleston were rather weak in their applications, the other writers of the group, Harte, Cable, Allen, Murfree, Freeman, and Garland, did some or all of their best work in it. Their experiments were not always successful, as shown, but the rate of success was much higher than that achieved in their other areas of setting experimentation.

[202] *Main-Travelled Roads*, 38.
[203] Ibid., 44.
[204] Ibid., 317.

4

SETTING PERSONIFIED

Human interest is an essential ingredient in fiction. In general, the closer the relationship between person and place, the more effective the story. It is only a short step from a setting which works in close relation to character to a setting which assumes, or usurps, the function of character. Though the local colorists had widely different techniques for bringing their landscapes alive, nearly all of them undertook some form of personification to intensify the human interest in their natural settings.

Bret Harte, in "The Luck of Roaring Camp", the story which opened up for him the nation's best magazines of fiction, devotes less space to descriptive matter than do his earlier stories, but nevertheless creates a more lively impression of setting. As Pattee noted, "M'liss" reveals "only here and there the wild California flavors", while in "The Luck of Roaring Camp" they are "the predominating characteristic".[1]

In "The Luck of Roaring Camp" the impression of a living scene grows throughout the text by an almost imperceptible progression. The fullest descriptive passage in the early part of the story is too brief to offer more than a glimpse of the scene:

> The camp lay in a triangular valley, between two hills and a river. The only outlet was a steep trail over the summit of a hill that faced the cabin, now illuminated by the rising moon. The suffering woman might have seen it from the rude bunk whereon she lay, – seen it winding like a silver thread until it was lost in the stars above.[2]

---

[1] Pattee, *American Short Story*, 233.
[2] *Novels and Stories*, I, 3-4.

Here the landscape is somewhat enlivened by the last sentence, which establishes the presence of an observer for whom the isolation of the camp has a practical meaning. The reader perceives that there is probably no outlet from Roaring Camp for the lonely creature except the road leading toward the stars. The scene, though not actually personified here, takes on a strong subjective interest which paves the way for further efforts in that direction. In a later passage the background begins to stir with excitement:

Above the swaying and moaning of the pines, the swift rush of the river, and the crackling of the fire, rose a sharp, querulous cry, – a cry unlike anything heard before in the camp. The pines stopped moaning, the river ceased to rush, and the fire to crackle. It seemed as if Nature had stopped to listen too.[3]

A still further step toward personification is taken in such passages as "Nature took the foundling [Luck] to her broader breast,"[4] or

Nature was his nurse and playfellow. For him she would let slip between the leaves golden shafts of sunlight that fell just within his grasp; she would send wandering breezes to visit him with the balm of hay and resinous gums; to him the tall red-woods nodded familiarly and sleepily, the bumble-bees buzzed, and the rooks cawed a slumbrous accompaniment.[5]

And finally, when Harte pictures the flood, the setting lives "in the confusion of rushing water, crushing trees, and crackling timber, and the darkness which seemed to flow with the water and blot out the fair valley".[6] There is never more than a glance at the background at any time, yet the setting as a whole is alive and predominant. There are no well-developed characters in the story; Cherokee Sal never speaks or stirs from her cot, the infant Luck is too young to have an individuality, and Stumpy is merely the representative man of Roaring Camp. It is the Camp itself that has real individuality; as the expressman reported,

"They've a street up there in 'Roaring' that would lay over any street in Red Dog. They've got rivers and flowers round their houses, and they

[3] Ibid., 4.
[4] Ibid., 9.
[5] Ibid., 15.
[6] Ibid., 17.

wash themselves twice a day. But they're mighty rough on strangers, and they worship an Ingin baby."[7]

Roaring Camp is interesting because it is vital, strange, and new. Its morality appears almost inverted, and its whole character is intelligible only because of its isolation and incongruous elements.

The setting techniques which Harte exhibited in "The Luck" were closely followed in those stories which succeeded it in the *Overland* within the next year and which were collected with it in the famous collection of 1870, *The Luck of Roaring Camp, and Other Sketches*.[8] The second story in this group was "The Outcasts of Poker Flat", taken from the January, 1869, issue of the *Overland*. Here the author is even more sparing in his descriptive passages than in "The Luck", but the hovering presence of a rugged nature is felt, especially since the outcasts are actually suffering from exposure to a winter snow storm. Three key descriptive passages may be selected for examination:

The spot was singularly wild and impressive. A wooded amphitheatre, surrounded on three sides by precipitous cliffs of naked granite, sloped gently toward the crest of another precipice that overlooked the valley.[9]

He [Oakhurst] looked at the gloomy walls that rose a thousand feet sheer above the circling pines around him; at the sky, ominously clouded; at the valley below, already deepening into shadow.[10]

As the shadows crept slowly up the mountain a slight breeze rocked the tops of the pine-trees, and moaned through their long and gloomy aisles.[11]

An ominous note is sounded and echoed by the use of such expressions as "wild and impressive" in the first selection; "gloomy", "ominously clouded", and "deepening into shadow" in the second; and "crept", "moaned", and "gloomy" in the third. Harte thus

[7] Ibid., 16.

[8] E. R. May, "Bret Harte and the *Overland Monthly*", *American Literature*, XXII (Nov., 1950), 260-71, believes Harte's "salaried leisure" while an editor on the *Overland* encouraged careful workmanship in his stories of this period, a quality lacking in his later stories when poverty drove him to hasty, careless work.

[9] *Novels and Stories*, I, 22.

[10] Ibid., 24.

[11] Ibid., 26.

plants emotional stimuli in the scene he is representing. The proximity of these short passages to characters mentioned almost in the same breath conveys the impression that perhaps these emotional qualities actually are intended to inhere in the characters, the nearest human observers. This interpretation is possible, since the emotional values are within the range of the characters. Though Harte assigned moods and feelings to natural objects, his intent must have been to portray the landscape as a sentient, volitional force. For example:

The third day came, and the sun, looking through the white-curtained valley, saw the outcasts divide their slowly decreasing store of provisions for the morning meal. It was one of the peculiarities of that mountain climate that its rays diffused a kindly warmth over the wintry landscape, as if in regretful commiseration of the past.

The wind lulled as if it feared to awaken them. Feathery drifts of snow, shaken from the long pine boughs, flew like white-winged birds, and settled about them as they slept. The moon through the rifted clouds looked down upon what had been the camp. But all human stain, all trace of earthly travail, was hidden beneath the spotless mantle mercifully flung from above.[12]

In these passages the sun, the wind, the moon, and the snow are personalities whose interests and sympathy are as real as those of the chorus in a Greek drama. Harte was continually trying to effect the heroic. Though he did not fully succeed, he was sometimes more powerful, if less sincere, as a result of the effort.

Behind the fateful disasters which terminate "The Luck" and "The Outcasts" there stands, in heroic stature, that particular Fate which rules the West, whose decree is sometimes capricious, often ironical, always final, by whose special whim the great snow snuffs out the lives of these outcasts of Poker Flat, just as the flood blots out the souls of Roaring Camp. A reason is never revealed – perhaps there is no justice nor purpose in these events – but at least there is freedom from the absurd morality of the social organization. In this story, Nature, the agent of that Fate, is herself kind and sympathetic, as she appears in nearly all of Harte's stories; but it is not possible for her to remain calm and "bucolic" in California, a land of vicissitude and hazard.

[12] Ibid., 31, 35.

"Tennessee's Partner" (*Overland,* October, 1869) is dominantly a character study, and the natural surroundings are even less frequently alluded to than in the preceding stories; yet they come into prominence nevertheless. Setting is managed by subtle implication, after the fashion of the two stories just discussed. No better example of the sympathy of natural objects can be found in all of Bret Harte's volumes than in this story. Though we are told that Nature has taken no cognizance of "that weak and foolish deed", the execution of Tennessee, we find that she is far from apathetic at the lonely grief of his honest, self-sacrificing partner:

The way led through Grizzley Canyon, – by this time clothed in funereal drapery and shadows. The red-woods, burying their moccasined feet in the red soil, stood in Indian-file along the track, trailing an uncouth benediction from their bending boughs upon the passing bier.[13]

Though Harte's successful stories are all characterized by a personalized setting, it does not follow that all of the stories in which he does personify the setting are artistically successful, for in some cases his technique seems to have lapsed sadly. Only moderately successful was "High-Water Mark", the first of Harte's Western stories to begin with setting. The four-page initial description of Dedlow Marsh attempts forthwith to personify this Western swamp almost as Thomas Hardy enlivens his famous Egdon Heath at the beginning of *The Return of the Native.* To quote in part,

When the tide was out on the Dedlow Marsh, its extended dreariness was patent. Its spongy, low-lying surface, sluggish inky pools, and tortuous sloughs, twisting their slimy way, eel-like, toward the open bay, were all hard facts. So were the few green tussocks, with their amphibious flavor, and unpleasant dampness....
The vocal expression of the Dedlow Marsh was also melancholy and depressing. The sepulchral boom of the bittern, the shriek of the curlew, the scream of passing brent, the wrangling of quarrelsome teal, the sharp, querulous protest of the startled crane, and a syllabled complaint of the "Killdeer" plover were beyond the power of written description.... But if Dedlow Marsh was cheerless at the slack of the low tide, you should have seen it when the tide was strong and full. When the damp air blew chilly over the cold, glittering expanse, and came to the faces of those who looked seaward like another tide; when a steel-like glint marked the low hollows

13 Ibid., 67-68.

and sinuous line of slough; when the great shell-incrusted trunks of fallen trees arose again, and went forth on their dreary, purposeless wanderings, drifting hither and thither...; when the fog came in with the tide and shut out the blue above, even as the green below had been obliterated; when boatmen, lost in that fog, paddling about in a hopeless way, started at what seemed the brushing of mermen's fingers on the boat's keel, or shrank from the tufts of grass spreading around like the floating hair of a corpse, and knew by these signs that they were lost upon Dedlow Marsh, and must make a night of it, and a gloomy one at that, – then you might know something of Dedlow Marsh at high water.[14]

With the setting thus presented directly and elaborately to the reader, Harte begins his narrative, a realistic, excited struggle of a mother to save herself and her infant in a devastating flood. The rapid succession of pictures in this story is not at all typical of Harte's better-known work. Rarely, in fact, has he pieced his material together so ineffectively. Not much happened, he writes, "considering the malevolent capacity of Dedlow Marsh"; and neither does much happen to the reader's interest. The dramatic potentialities are ignored; the Marsh as a personal force loses rather than gains in credibility. For an inanimate object like the Marsh to assume a character role, a prolonged initial description is of far less value than a gradually developed personification, such as Harte employs in the stories mentioned above.

A story which exhibits the same poor setting technique as "High-Water Mark" is "The Twins of Table Mountain" (1879). This story opens with a characterization of Table Mountain, which "seemed to lie so near the quiet, passionless stars that at night it caught something of their calm remoteness".[15] Near the beginning of the story the mountain stands unique and powerful, fully capable of dominating forthcoming events. But once the plot situation is developed, the setting interest loses out to melodrama. The meticulous representation of Table Mountain, which has little or no function, is disproportionately prolonged.

The personification of nature was a deeply rooted habit in Harte's literary mind, as may be seen even in his minor uses of this device. Scattered through his stories are frequent sketches of Nature,

14 Ibid., 67-68, 107-109.
15 *Writings*, III, 123.

always with a capital *N*, posing as incarnations of landscapes or scenes:

Thankful went early to bed and cried herself to sleep. And Nature, possibly, followed her example, for at sunset a great thaw set in.[16]

In the wild and lawless arms of Nature herself we found an embrace as clinging, as hopeless and restraining, as the civilization from which we had fled.[17]

A quiet that might have come from the lingering influence of the still virgin solitude around it, as if Nature had forgotten the intrusion, or were stealthily retaking her own.[18]

The great Mother raised herself to comfort them with smiling hillsides, or encompassed them and drew them closer in the saving arms of her mountains.[19]

Perhaps the giant mountains recognized some kin in him, and fed and strengthened him after their own fashion.[20]

One by one the great snow-peaks slowly arose behind them, lifting themselves, as if to take a last wondering look at the man they had triumphed over, but had not subdued.[21]

"A little shock of earthquake", he said blandly; "a mere thrill! I think", he added with a faint smile, "we may say that Nature herself has applauded our efforts in good old California fashion, and signified her assent".[22]

Some eccentricity of Nature or circumstance was invariably starting up in his daily path to the schoolroom…. If Nature was thus capricious with his elders, why should folk think it strange if she was as mischievous with a small boy?[23]

It is impossible to determine at what point the figurative gives way to the mythopoeic. The "Nature" that is brought to life for the brief duration of a figure is something quite different from "Nature" which rules continuously and with incontrovertible power over the lives of the puppets in its reach. The preceding quotations taken out of context would suggest that Harte consis-

---

[16] "Thankful Blossom", *Writings*, X, 1.
[17] "Captain Jim's Friend", ibid., V, 370.
[18] "A Maecenas of the Pacific Slope", ibid., VII, 158.
[19] "A Night on the Divide", ibid., XV, 292-93.
[20] "The Man and the Mountain", ibid., XVI, 260.
[21] Ibid., 266.
[22] "The Youngest Miss Piper", ibid., XVII, 137.
[23] "An Ali Baba of the Sierras", ibid., 329.

tently entertained a conception of Nature as a constant, omnipotent observer of humanity, usually sympathetic but at times capricious. Seldom is this impression actually developed in a story. His literary method was far from scientific; on the whole he was more subjective than objective as an artist. He could not be called a mystic, yet he was prone, at least among the more exalted realms of nature, to feel spirit behind matter. His scenes are charged with a life beneath the surface, ready to assume as much humanity as the reader's credulity can accept.

In Twain's stories, as might be expected, there is only a slight suggestion of personification, far less than in Bret Harte's. In *Roughing It* he pictures living mountains:

a convention of Nature's kings that stood ten, twelve, and even thirteen thousand feet high – grand old fellows who would have to stoop to see Mt. Washington, in the twilight....

These Sultans of the fastnesses were turbaned with tumbled volumes of cloud, which shredded away from time to time and drifted off fringed and torn, trailing their continents of shadow after them; and catching presently on an intercepting peak, wrapped about it and brooded there – then shredded away again and left the purple peak, as they had left the purple domes, downy and white with new-laid snow. In passing, the monstrous rays of cloud hung low and swept right along over the spectator's head, swinging their tatters so nearly in his face that his impulse was to shrink when they came closest.[24]

In short stories, however, Mark Twain abstains from personifications of this sort – that is, except for purposes of burlesque. In his playful "The Enemy Conquered" the heroine sheds "silent tears" which "mingle with the waves, and take a last farewell of their agitated home, to seek a peaceful dwelling among the rolling floods".[25] The hero addresses his beloved natural rendezvous with a rhetoric as declamatory as Pyramus' lines to Wall:

Oh, ye scenes forever glorious, ye celebrated scenes, ye renowned spot of my hymnal moments; how replete is your chart with sublime reflections![26]

In his beautiful wood the dawn comes as "the harbinger of a

24 *Roughing It*, I, 103.
25 *Works*, X, 178.
26 Ibid., 153.

fair and prosperous day", and at evening "gloomy twilight... lay heavily on the Indian Plains". Also "the mountain air breathed fragrance" over the eminence and "a rosy tinge rested on the glassy waters that murmured at its base".[27] Twain doubtless classed pathetic fallacy with other forms of irrelevancy and ostentation. The inconsistency between his theory of abstention and his occasional indulgence is one of the many puzzles of Twain's genius.

Cable, like Harte, has a habit of endowing nature with human characteristics in descriptive figures of speech. Though Cable's figures are more frequent and more compelling in the early *Scribner's* stories than in his later work, there are two subjects which he was particularly prone to personify, and which he usually could personify with complete success: natural objects and houses.

As far as nature is concerned, Cable's religio-theological concepts led him to sense a mind and spirit, or Providence, within physical forms. He was not, strictly speaking, a pantheist, though to him, as to Gregory in "The Solitary",

sea, sky, book, island, and...humanity, all seemed part of one whole, and all to speak together in one harmony, while they toiled together for one harmony some day to be perfected.[28]

Cable feels too deeply the influence of landscapes to grant that they are mechanisms; to him, as to Bonaventure, "in God's religion is comprise' the total mechanique of civilization".[29] Figures in Cable's stories approaching personification are not uncommon:

One beautiful summer night...all nature seemed hushed in ecstasy.[30]

One could get glimpses of the gardens in Fraubourg Ste.-Marie standing in silent wretchedness, so many tearful Lucretias, tattered victims of the storm.[31]

The sun seemed to come out and work for the people.[32]

The seasons were as inexorable at Grande Pointe as elsewhere, but there was no fierceness in them. The very frosts were gentle. Slowly and kindly

---

[27] Ibid., 131-132.
[28] *Strong Hearts* (New York, 1908), 42.
[29] *Bonaventure*, 186.
[30] "Madame Delphine", *Old Creole Days*, 40.
[31] "Posson Jone'", *Old Creole Days*, 150.
[32] Ibid., 163.

they stripped the green robes from many a thicket, ejected like defaulting tenants the blue linnet, the orchard oriole, the non-pareil...[33]

All nature in glad, gay earnest.[34]

Our old friend the mocking-bird, neglecting his faithful wife and letting his house go to decay, kept dropping in, all hours of the day, tasting the berries' rank pulp, stimulating, stimulating, drowning care, you know,... and going home in the evening scolding and swaggering, and getting to bed barely able to hang on the roost.[35]

How beautiful, how gentle was Nature after her transport of passion![36]

Cable's personification of houses, especially those of older architecture, is generally effective. "Age gives poetry to a house", he once remarked, "though a house well married to a good landscape gets at once some guise of matronly years, if only a sweet step-motherly dignity and benevolence."[37]

Many of Cable's houses are so highly individualized, as, for instance, Jean-ah Poquelin's, that they assume personality. For example:

a small, low brick house of a story and a half, set out upon the sidewalk, as weather-beaten and mute as an aged beggar fallen asleep.[38]

The discolored stucco... keeps dropping off into the garden as though the old cafe was stripping for the plunge into oblivion – disrobing for its execution.[39]

With its gray stucco peeling off in broad patches, it has a solemn look of gentility in rags, and stands, or, as it were, hangs about the corner of two ancient streets, like a faded fop who pretends to be looking for employment.[40]

A peep through one of the shops reveals... rotten staircases that seem vainly trying to clamber out of the rubbish.[41]

A decaying cornice hangs over, dropping its bits of mortar on passers below, like a boy at a boarding school.[42]

[33] *Bonaventure*, 103.
[34] Ibid., 116.
[35] Ibid., 180-181.
[36] Ibid., 291.
[37] "Speculations of a Story-Teller", *Atlantic Monthly*, LXXVII, 95 (July, 1896).
[38] "Madame Delphine", *Old Creole Days*, 3.
[39] "Cafe des Exiles", *Old Creole Days*, 85.
[40] "'Sieur George", *Old Creole Days*, 247.
[41] Ibid.
[42] Ibid., 248.

The four-story brick got old and ugly, and the surroundings dim and dreary.[43]

The houses of Rue Royale gave a start and rattled their windows. In the long, irregular line of balconies the beauty of the city rose up. Then the houses jumped again and the windows rattled.[44]

One of the most sophisticated personifiers of landscape was Mary Noailles Murfree. As the *Atlantic* reviewer of *In The Tennessee Mountains* pointed out, "the mountain solitudes... assume the function of *dramatis personae*"; "in this utilization of forces not human, Mr. Craddock is not surpassed by any writer of his time".[45] In Harte's sustained personifications, it will be remembered, a landscape is generally individualized and vitalized as a whole, gradually drawing its breath of life from the cumulative effect of successive details, brief and well distributed throughout the story. With Murfree, on the other hand, particular landscape objects, mountains, cliffs, or forests, are more likely to be personified than the background as a whole, and her successive descriptions are cumulative in their impression but seldom brief.

In "Drifting Down Lost Creek" the lonely little stream not only symbolizes Cynthia Ware's frustration and loss of hope, but also serves as a companion in her loneliness and a counselor in her despondence. The girl feels her life hopelessly hemmed in by the surrounding Cumberland range:

It seemed... that nothing which went beyond this barrier ever came back again. One by one the days passed over it, and in splendid apotheosis, in purple and crimson and gold, they were received into the heavens, and returned no more.... She often watched the floating leaves, a nettle here and there, the broken wing of a moth, and wondered whither these trifles were borne, on the elegiac current. She came to fancy that her life was like them, worthless in itself and without a mission; drifting down Lost Creek, to vanish vaguely in the Mountains.[46]

In her utter dejection, Cynthia revisits the stream for a final communion and observes that "before it takes its desperate plunge into the unexplored caverns of the mountains, Lost Creek lends

[43] Ibid., 253-54.
[44] "Madame Delicieuse", *Old Creole Days*, 276.
[45] "An American Story Writer", *Atlantic Monthly*, LIV, 131-33 (July, 1884).
[46] *In the Tennessee Mountains*, 1-2.

its aids to diverse jobs of very prosaic work".[47] She decides to emulate Lost Creek's example, and her remaining years are like "the floating leaves drifting down Lost Creek", until at last "she ceases to question and regret, and bravely does the work nearest at hand".[48]

In "Over on T'Other Mounting" the setting again usurps the function of character. The hint of superstitious credulity in some of the other stories here becomes a central theme. "T'Other Mounting" is vaguely in ill repute among its neighbors, its bad name coming from its being "the onluckiest place ennywhar nigh about". Its personality is individual and striking, as the descriptions ably demonstrate:

The great masses of gray rock, jutting out... here and there, wore a darkly frowning aspect.[49]

The T'Other Mountain was all a dusk, sad purple under the faintly pulsating stars, save that high along the horizontal line of its summit gleamed the strange red radiance of the dead and gone sunset.... Here and there the uncanny light streamed through bare limbs of an early leafless tree, which looked in the distance like some bony hand beckoning, or warning, or raised in horror.[50]

A late hunter, driven by necessity to the dreaded place, falls into its clutches, and the gloom and mysteries of the mountain cast him into superstitious terror. Spirits make him spiteful, and his mind reverts to his old grudges; becoming desperate and unable to injure his real persecutor, he attempts to murder a neighbor whom he dislikes while the latter is returning from a late errand. His act is not detected, but he continues to look upon the mountain with horror. Its changing aspects fascinate him, enthrall him, and gradually drive him mad. The culminating tableau of "T'Other Mounting" is effected by combining a burning forest with an electrical storm at night. A few lines will suggest the weird melee:

Across the dark slope of the mountain below, flashes of lightning were shooting in zig-zag lines, and wherever they gleamed were seen those frantic

[47] Ibid., 2.
[48] Ibid., 79.
[49] Ibid., 258.
[50] Ibid., 260.

skeleton hands raised and wrung in anguish. It was cruel sport for the cruel winds; they maddened over gorge and cliff and along wooded steeps, carrying far upon their wings the sparks of desolation. From the summit, myriads of jets of flame reached up to the placid stars; about the base of the mountain lurked a lake of liquid fire, with wreaths of blue smoke hovering over it; ever and anon, athwart the slope darted the sudden lightning, widening into sheets of flame.[51]

A third striking example of setting as character is the evil cliff in "The Mystery of Witch-Face Mountain" (1895). It is a "great gaunt bare space showing the face of ill omen, sibylline, sinister, definite indeed".[52] From afar off it can be seen, "silently mowing and grimacing at the world below,... marking this as an unlucky day".[53] "One dark night", Constant Hite relates,

Ez that Hanway fambly war settin' on the porch... the daughter, Narcissa by name, she calls out," Look! Look! I see the witch-face!"... and thar, ez true ez life, war the witch-face glimmerin' in the midst o' the black night, and agrinnin' at 'em an' a-mockin' at 'em, and lighted up ez ef by fire.[54]

Again, while the jury of view was crossing through the woods after dark,

the witch-face glared down at them from the dense darkness of the woods. The quick chilly repulsion of the strangers as they gazed spell-bound at the apparition was outmatched by the horror of those who had known the fantasy from childhood; – never thus had they beheld the gaunt old face! What strange unhallowed mystery was this, that it should smile and grimace and mock at them from out the shadowy night, with flickers of light as of laughter running athwart its grisly lineaments? What evil might it portend?[55]

A second way in which personified objects function in Murfree's stories is as a foil to human actions, or as a vociferous chorus that intensifies the mood of a scene by repeating or accentuating the dominant impression. With most local colorists this use is usually limited to a single figure of speech, but Murfree maintains her choruses by repeated references. In "A-Playin' of Old Sledge at

[51] Ibid., 275.
[52] *The Mystery of Witch-Face Mountain*, 8.
[53] Ibid., 9.
[54] Ibid., 20-21.
[55] Ibid., 132.

the Settlemint" (1884), the personification of the surroundings begins with a portrayal of the echoes from the card game:

There was a subtle weird influence in those exultant tones, rising and falling by fitful starts in that tangled, wooded desert, now loud and close at hand, now the faintest whisper of a sound. The men all turned their slow eyes toward the sombre shadows, so black beneath the silver moon, and then looked at each other.[56]

The old hunter is the first to become excited. "Whenever I hear them critters a-laffin' that thar way in them woods I puts out fur home an bars up the door, fur I hev hearn tell ez how the sperits air a-prowlin' round there, an' some mischief is a-happenin'."[57] Later in the evening "the single spectator of the game...glanced over his shoulder at the dark trees whence the hidden mimic of the woods, with some strong suggestion of sinister intent, repeated the agitated tones" of the players.[58] As the game advances, the echoes become even more definite and pronounced.

"Lord in heaven!" rang loud from the depths of the dark woods. "Heaven!" softly vibrated the distant heights. The crags close at hand clanged back the sound, and the air was filled with repetitions of the word, growing fainter and fainter, till they might have seemed the echo of a whisper.[59]

When a struggle arose, and the store-keeper cried "Fight!" into the darkness, "the affrighted rocks rang with the frenzied cry, and the motionless woods and the white moonlight seemed pervaded with myriads of strange, uncanny voices".[60] The principal character, Wray, showed on his features and in his character the "indefinable tinge of sadness that rests upon the Allegheny wilds, that hovers about the mountaintops, that broods over the silent woods, that sounds in the voice of the singing waters";[61] yet the landscape itself is also made to reflect his own particular changes of mood. While he is angry and confused the clouds linger upon the mountaintop; but when peace and new-born resolution come to him during his tramp through the country, the clouds disperse, the

[56] *In the Tennessee Mountains*, 97.
[57] Idem.
[58] Ibid., 102.
[59] Ibid., 107.
[60] Ibid., 90.
[61] Ibid., 90.

mist is "broken into thousands of fleecy white wreaths, clinging to the fantastically tinted foliage, ...the sunlight...striking deep into the valley".[62]

In the last story of the famous collection, "The 'Harnt' that Walks Chilhowee" (1883), the ghostly feeling experienced by the girl is largely supported by the utterances of a personified nature which surrounds her. For example,

Noiseless wings flitted through the dusk; now and then the bats swept by so close as to wave Clarsie's hair with the wind of their flight. What airy, glittering, magical thing was that gigantic spider-web suspended between the silver moon and her shining eyes! Ever and anon there came from the woods a strange, weird, long-drawn sigh, unlike the stir of the wind in the trees, unlike the fret of the water on the rocks. Was it the voiceless sorrow of the sad earth?[63]

This impression is renewed later in the story by more "sweeping of the bat's dusky wings", which was "a part of the night's witchery".[64] Again, while she is alone in a mountain path,

There was no sound in the house, and from the dark woods arose only monotonous voices of the night, so familiar to her ears that she accounted their murmurous iteration as silence too.[65]

No chirp of half-awakened bird, no tapping of woodpecker, or the mysterious death-watch but far along the dewy aisles of the forest, the ungrateful Spot...lifted up her voice, and set the echoes vibrating.[66]

Presently she hears the ghost, "the quick beat of hastening footsteps, the sobbing sound of panting breath", and sees him pass between her and the sinking moon. A party of horsemen speed by and "the rocks and the steeps were hilarious with the sound".[67] On her second visit to the hiding place of the ghost it is almost morning, and the strange Presences about her are again almost silent, but none the less impressive:

It was all very still, very peaceful, almost holy. One could hardly believe that these consecrated solitudes had once reverberated with the echoes of man's death-dealing ingenuity, and that Reuben Crabb had fallen, shot

[62] Ibid., 117.
[63] Ibid., 291-92.
[64] Ibid., 305.
[65] Ibid., 306.
[66] Ibid., 308.
[67] Ibid., 309.

through and through, amid that wealth of flowers at the forks of the road. She heard suddenly the faraway baying of a hound. Her great eyes dilated, and she lifted her head to listen. Only the solemn silence of the woods, the slow sinking of the noiseless moon, the voiceless splendor of that eloquent day-star.[68]

More frequently, Murfree's personified choruses are winds or waterfalls. In "The Moonshiners at Hoho-Hebee Falls" (1895), Nehemiah Yerby enters a remote region, guided solely by the "wild, sweet, woodland voice" of Hide-and-Seek Creek. "What affinity this brawling vagrant [the creek] had for the briars and the rocks and the tangled fastnesses!" In fact, he could scarcely "press into its banks and look down upon its dimpled, laughing, heedless face"[69] without having his flesh torn by thorns. After this fragmentary character role, Hide-and-Seek Creek joins the mighty choral arrangement in which all the voices of nature are blended into a

fine sylvan symphony of the sound of falling water – the tinkling bell-like tremors of its lighter tones mingling with the sonorous, continuous, deeper theme rising from its weight and volume and movement; with the occasional cry of a wild bird deep in the new verdure of the forests striking through the whole with a brilliant, incidental, detached effect.... The wild minstrelsy of the woods felt no lack, and stream and wind and harping pine and vagrant bird lifted their voices in their wonted strains.[70]

This music flows ceaselessly through the remainder of the story, and plays the accompaniment to Yerby's excitements and moods. While he is held a fearful captive by the moonshiners, "clear-eyed day" is replaced by night, "with mystery and doubt and dark presage", and

The voice of Hobo-hebee Falls seemed to him louder, full of strange, uncomprehended meanings and insistent iteration. Vague echoes were elicited. Sometimes in a seeming pause he could catch their lisping sibilant tones repeating, repeating – what? As the darkness encroached yet more heavily upon the cataract, the sense of its unseen motion so close at hand oppressed his very soul; it gave an idea of the swift gathering of shifting invisible multitudes, coming and going – who could say whence or whither?[71]

[68] Ibid., 315.
[69] *The Phantoms of the Foot-Bridge*, 234.
[70] Ibid., 243.
[71] Ibid., 254.

These selections, because of their fragmentary quality, indicate only partially the manner in which Murfree brings her landscape to life. Except for an occasional pathetic fallacy, her artistic restraint saves her from mawkishness and sentimentality, the natural effects of personifications with too little room for imagination. Murfree is generally subtle enough as a mythopoeic technician to personify nature through the superstitious minds of the mountain folk. Her earlier stories employing personifications, such as "Drifting Down Lost Creek", "Over on T'Other Mounting", "A-Playin' of Old Sledge at the Settlemint", and "The Harnt' that Walks Chilhowee", are superior to the stories of about a decade later. "The Mystery of Witch-Face Mountain" and "The Moonshiners of Hoho-Hebee Falls", mainly for reasons of proportion and structure, are not easily illustrated in brief quotations. So much dead descriptive matter is included in later tales that the illusion of personification is generally dissipated.

Nowhere in Page's formula was there a provision for personified settings. The strong sentiment that Page sometimes attaches to details of setting is almost always understood as belonging within the imagination of the characters, and not inhering in the objects themselves. Among the entire Southern group Page is perhaps the freest from pathetic fallacy, his style being almost too simple for even purely figurative personifications. Perhaps he comes closest to personifications in his descriptions of haunted places, such as No Haid Pawn, which "stood... all undisturbed and unchanging"[72] at the beginning of the story, and at the end "reclaimed its own, and the spot with all its secrets lay buried under its dark waters".[73] In "The Christmas Peace" appears a winding creek which "is as ungovernable as a Hamden's temper", for "on the mere pretext of a thunder-storm, it would burst forth from its banks, tear the fences to pieces, and even change its course".[74] In "Elsket" the creeks are even more energetic; in this story

several little streams came jumping down as white as milk from the glaciers stuck between the mountain tops, and after resting in two or three tiny

[72] *In Old Virginia*, 164.
[73] Ibid., 186.
[74] *Bred in the Bone* (New York, 1904), 187.

lakes which looked like hand-mirrors lying in the grass below, went bub-
bling and foaming on the edge of the precipice, over which they sprang, to
be dashed into vapor and snow hundreds of feet down.[75]

In "Miss Godwin's Inheritance" midwinter nature is half-heartedly
personified: "having arrayed herself in immaculate garb", she
"seems well content to rest and survey her work".[76] Later in the
same story "Spring announces that she has come to pay you a visit,
and leaves her visiting card in bluebirds and dandelions."[77] But
such examples are far too rare to be accounted a part of Page's
narrative style.

Allen carries the personification of Nature farther than does almost
any other American writer of prose fiction. His tendency to bring
his background to life has already been apparent in the selections
used in preceding chapters. From 1888 onward Nature appears as
a character in almost every story which Allen wrote, at first usually
in a minor role as sympathizer and companion to her kindred human fellows, and later as an apathetic, willful, omnipotent Force,
working upon all creatures both externally and internally and
determining even their private desires. There is an inescapable
inconsistency in Allen's characterization of Nature in most stories,
for she assumes, like the people in fairy stories, many different
forms. In the same story she may appear as the whole cosmic
creation, of which man is a part; as a life-like parent or companion
to a character; or as an inscrutable intellect which controls all natural objects – her automata – including man.

The more poetic side of Allen's literary disposition seems to be
moving him toward mysticism or pantheism, but at the same time
his scientific and intellectual nature inclines him toward emergent
evolution and scientific positivism. Without settling even in his
own mind the problems arising from this conflict, he continued to
show the possibility of the scientific point of view in short fiction
without completely surrendering the well-proved values of an Unknown. At the conclusion of "Summer in Arcady", for example,
after Allen has proved that man is essentially an animal and that

[75] *Elsket*, 16.
[76] *Under the Crust*, 10.
[77] Ibid., 27.

his basic impulses have nothing to do with institutions and morality, he backs down after Hilary's marriage to speak of the "rays of that divine light of the spirit which also rests upon such a union", and the "fresh vision of the real manliness of what is right".[78]

In Allen's earlier stories, it has been pointed out, personified natural objects, or nature, generally assume the role of sympathetic companion. In "The White Cowl", while Father Paleman sits at rest in the garden,

Nature was in ecstasy. The sunlight never fell more joyous upon the uplifting shadows of human life. The breeze that cooled his sweating face was heavy with the odor of the wonderful monastery roses…. All the liquid air was slumbrous with the minute music of insect life and from the honeysuckles clambering over the wall at his back came the murmur of the happy, happy bees.[79]

In "Sister Dolorosa", "the very landscape, barren and dead… spoke to the beholder the everlasting poetry of the race".[80] The little nun makes long, poetic addresses to the white violet, her "pure-souled" "little Sister"; to the English sparrow, "not a bird, but a little brown mendicant friar, begging barefoot in the snow"; to a butterfly, "fragile Psyche, mute and perishable lover of the gorgeous earth".[81] With Helm, on the other hand,

always the presence of the convent made itself felt over the landscape, dominating it, solitary and impregnable…. It appeared to watch him; to have an eye at every window; to see in him a lurking danger.[82]

In the transition stories, such as "A Kentucky Cardinal" and its sequel, "Aftermath", the personifications of Nature are innumerable. The idea of her companionship with man is continued, but she begins to show herself more sincere and beautiful than humanity, which is always fraught with imperfections. The central character and narrator must therefore grant the inferiority of human companions as compared to birds and trees. "The only being in the universe at which I ever snarled", he says, "or with which I

[78] *Summer in Arcady*, 167.
[79] *Flute and Violin*, 138.
[80] Ibid., 176.
[81] Ibid., 194-95.
[82] Ibid., 228.

ever rolled over in the mud and fought like a common cur, is man."[83] Later on he remarks that "it is a pleasure to chronicle the beginning of an acquaintanceship between his proud eminence the young cardinal and myself".[84] So compelling does this friendship become that Adam at first refuses point blank to betray his little feathered friend even to win the woman he loves. In "Aftermath" a love triangle appears with Adam, Georgiana, and Nature (in the guise of a redbird) as the three extremities. After Adam's marriage his wife is jealous of his love of the woods and confides in her husband her fear that he will wander off like Thoreau or Audubon.

Every spring nature will be just as young to you [she says]; I shall be always older. The water you love ripples, never wrinkles. I shall cease rippling and begin wrinkling. No matter what happens, each summer the birds get fresh feathers; only think how my old ones will never drop out.[85]

Adam explains to her the qualities of nature that have won his admiration and love:

When I study nature there are no delicate or dangerous or forbidden subjects. The trees have no evasions. The weeds are honest. Running water is not trying to escape. The sunsets are not colored with hypocrisy. The lightning is not revenge. Everything stands forth in the sincerity of its being, and nature invites me to exercise the absolute liberty of my mind upon all life.[86]

You may never study human life as you study nature. With men you must take your choice: liberty for your mind and a prison for your body; liberty for your body and a prison for your mind.[87]

The relationship between Adam and Nature is not so much that of lover and mistress, or that of masculine comradeship, as it is that of child and maternal parent:

It is as if Nature had spread out her last loveliness and said: "See! You have before you now all that you can get from me! It is not enough. Realize this in time. I am your Mother. Love me as a child. But remember: such love can be only a little part of your life."[88]

[83] *A Kentucky Cardinal and Aftermath*, 7.
[84] Ibid., 87.
[85] Ibid., 197.
[86] Ibid., 211-12.
[87] Ibid., 214.
[88] Ibid., 69.

Nature is sometimes the "old Nurse", insisting that the spring evergreen still wear its "frosted nightcap"; sometimes she is an energetic housekeeper, whom Adam loves to see doing

her spring house cleaning in Kentucky, with the rain clouds for her water buckets and the winds for her brooms. What an amount of drenching and sweeping she can do in a day! How she dashes pailful and pailful into every corner, till the whole earth is as clean as a new floor! Another day she attacks the pile of dead leaves, where they have lain since last October, and scatters them in a trice, so that every cranny may be sunned and aired. Or, grasping her long brooms by the handles, she will go into the woods and beat the icicles off the big trees as a house wife would brush down cobwebs.... This done, she begins to hang up soft new curtains at the forest windows, and to spread over her floor a new carpet of emerald loveliness such as no mortal looms could ever have woven. And then, at last, she sends out invitations through the South, and even to some tropical lands, for the birds to come and spend the summer in Kentucky. The invitations are sent out in March, and accepted in April and May, and by June her house is full of visitors.[89]

Adam's affection for his friends of the woods, even for that "august antiquarian", the old oak to be used for firewood, is temporarily eclipsed by his love for Georgiana, but after her death he returns pathetically to his earlier love:

As I approached the edge of the forest, it was as though an invisible company of the influences came gently to meet me and sought to draw me back into their old friendship. I found myself stroking the trunks of trees as I would throw my arm around the shoulders of a tired comrade; I drew down the branches and plunged my face into the new leaves as into a tonic stream.[90]

In "A Kentucky Cardinal" and "Aftermath" Nature merely uses beauty and friendship to entice living things to fulfill her purposes, but in "Summer in Arcady" she becomes no longer a companion to man but an absolute and inconsiderate dictator. Human volition is reduced to an illusion, as Nature reveals her aim:

"These blindfolded children! they think they are giving a picnic; they do not see that it is mine. They do not look around and behold with terror how I have called back to me nearly all their grandfathers and grandmothers; that I am about done with their fathers and mothers; and that their

89 Ibid., 20-21.
90 Ibid., 252-53.

whole land – these rich old homesteads, these fields with herds and flocks, these crops, and orchards, and gardens – would soon become a waste unless I gave picnics and the like, from which I always gather fresh generations and keep things going. *I* will be at this picnic."[91]

At the picnic she again reveals her character in this advice: "Go it, my children!... Dance away! Whatever is natural is right."[92] At this time of the year

Nature is lashing everything – grass, fruit, insects, cattle, human creatures – more fiercely onward to the fulfilment of her ends. She is the great heartless haymaker, wasting not a ray of sunshine or a clod, but caring naught for the light that beats upon a throne, and holding man and woman, with their longing for immortality and their caprices for joy and pain, as of no more account than a couple of fertilizing nasturtiums.[93]

With Allen's experimentations the role of personified nature was elevated from that of a mere chorus or malevolent influence in Murfree's stories to that of intimate companion, mistress, or great Dame ruling with imperious domination. The difficulties which Allen encountered are reflected in the unfavorable notices of his work. A reviewer of "Summer in Arcady" wrote in the *Saturday Review*:

Nature, with a big N, and in so many letters, is flung at us on every page, until we are sick of her, until we are forced into an attitude of hostility, and would almost quarrel with a perfectly acceptable thesis out of sheer annoyance.[94]

In making Nature the chief personality in a story, Allen was obliged to reaffirm throughout the story the impression of her as a real character, though never a very satisfactory one. Nature is not entirely devoid of human interest but cannot function as a character in a drama of real suspense because of the inconsistencies in the point of view from which Allen presents her to the reader.

A large majority of Jewett's[95] short stories are mere descriptive sketches of scenes and people, yet they are seldom deficient in human interest. "It is but seldom, as yet", she realized, "that

[91] *Summer in Arcady*, 30.
[92] Ibid., 32.
[93] Ibid., 86-87.
[94] "A Summer in Arcady", *Saturday Review*, LXXXIII, 204 (February 20, 1897).
[95] A part of this section has previously appeared in "Sarah Orne Jewett and 'The Palpable Present Intimate'", *Colby Library Quarterly*, VIII (September, 1968), 146-55.

people really care much for anything for its own sake, until it is
proved to have some connection with human-kind."[96] She does
not allow her descriptive muse to stray from the character situation, as do some local colorists. Skilled at creating human interest
by personifying natural objects, Jewett showed an advancement
in two respects at least: first, she breathed life, so to speak, into the
most omnipresent of natural objects, the New England trees and
flowers; second, she aroused a deep sympathy for these creations
by assuming a fresh and personal companionship with them in an
intimate, unaffected style like Henry Thoreau's.

Jewett's personifications of local fauna and flora are reminiscent
of Allen's best work minus the symbolism, but she is superior to
him in constancy of viewpoint. She wrote to Mrs. Fields at various
times that "hepaticas are like some people, very dismal blue, with
cold hands and faces"; that "There is nothing dearer than a trig
little company of anemones in a pasture, all growing close together
as if they kept each other warm, and wanted the whole sun to
themselves besides"; that she is "neighborly with the hop-toads"
and "intimate with a big poppy"; and that she has been carrying
on a sort of silent intrigue with "a very handsome little bee" who
"understands things" and knows she "can do him no harm".[97] In
"Cunner-Fishing", a Deephaven sketch, she has one of her characters observe

That the more one lives out of doors the more personality there seems to be
in what we call inanimate things. The strength of the hills and the voice of
the waves are no longer only grand poetical sentences, but an expression of
something real....[98]

There is no end of strange personalities among Jewett's trees.
"In Shadow", another Deephaven piece, contains a description
of some gnarled pitch-pines which

looked like a band of outlaws; they were such wild-looking trees. They
seemed very old, and as if their savage fights with the winter winds had
made them hardhearted.[99]

[96] *Country By-Ways*, 4.
[97] *Letters of Sarah Orne Jewett*, ed. Annie Fields (Boston, 1911), 41, 45, 119.
[98] *Deephaven*, 186-87.
[99] Ibid., 206.

The pines in "A Bit of Shore Life" (1879):

ifted their heads proudly against the blue sky,... and I admired them as much as they could have expected. They must have been a landmark for many miles to the westward, for they grew on high land, and they could pity, from a distance, any number of their poor relations who were just able to keep body and soul together, and had grown up thin and hungry in the crowded woods. But, though their lower branches might snap and crackle at a touch, their tops were brave and green, and they kept up appearances, at any rate, these poorer pines.[100]

Also there were

four jolly old apple trees,...which looked as if they might be the last of a once flourishing orchard. They were standing in a row, in exactly the same position, with their heads thrown gayly back, as if they were all dancing in an old-fashioned reel; and, after the forward and back, one might expect them to turn partners gallantly. I laughed aloud when I caught sight of them; there was something very funny in their looks, so jovial and whole-hearted, with a sober, cheerful pleasure, as if they gave their whole minds to it. It was like some old gentlemen and ladies who catch the spirit of the thing, and dance with the rest at a Christmas party.[101]

The narrator is especially partial to a family group of poplars:

a little procession of a father and mother and three or four children out for an afternoon walk, coming down through the field to the river. As you rowed up or down they stood up in bold relief against the sky, for they were on high land. I was deeply attached to them, and in the spring, when I went down the river for the first time, they were always covered with the first faint green mist of their leaves, and it seemed as if they had been watching for me, and thinking that perhaps I might go by that afternoon.[102]

In "A Winter Drive" (1881):

The white birches look out of season, as if they were still wearing their summer clothes, and the wretched larches which stand on the edges of the swamps look as if they had been intended for evergreens, but had been somehow unlucky, and were in destitute circumstances. It seems as if the pines and hemlocks ought to show Christian charity to those sad and freezing relations.[103]

---

[100] *Old Friends and New*, 253.
[101] Ibid., 254.
[102] *Country By-Ways*, 30.
[103] Ibid., 164.

The narrator's particular friend is a

> solitary tree which is a great delight to me, and I go to pay it an afternoon visit every now and then, far away from the road across some fields and pastures. It is an ancient pitch-pine, and it grows beside a spring, and has acres of room to lord it over. It thinks everything of itself, and although it is an untidy house-keeper, and flings its dry twigs and sticky cones all around the short grass underneath, I have a great affection for it.... The old tree is very wise, it sees that much of the world's business is great foolishness, and yet when I have been a fool myself and wander away out of doors to think it over, I always find a more cheerful atmosphere, and a more sensible aspect to my folly, under the shadow of this friend of mine.[104]

"Farmer Finch" (1885) contains some very striking tree-folk:

> As one caught sight of the solemn audience of black and gloomy cedars that seemed to have come together to stand on the curving hill-sides, one instinctively looked down at the leveled arena of marsh-land below, half fearing to see some awful sacrificial site or silent combat. It might be an angry company of hamadryads who had taken the shape of cedar-trees on this day of revenge and terror.... The little trees stood beside their elders in families, solemn and stern.[105]

In "A Neighbor's Landmark" (1894), which has more plot than most Jewett stories, two tall pines play a silent character role of considerable importance. They have been serviceable in guiding seamen into port; "they felt their responsibility as landmarks and sentinels".[106] In a weak moment Chauncery Packer forgets how they have served his people and his ancestors and sells them to a conscienceless lumberman. The community circulates a petition to save the lives of the Packer Pines, but in the meantime old Packer himself regrets his sudden promise and rows home across the bay just in time to prevent their "murder".

> "I should miss them old trees", he said; "they always make me think of a married couple. They ain't no common growth, be they, Joe? Everybody knows 'em. I bet you if anything happened to one on 'em t'other would go an' die. They say ellums has mates, an' all them big trees."[107]

Jewett's bird and flower characters are so much overshadowed

104 Ibid., 179.
105 *A White Heron and Other Stories*, 38.
106 *The Life of Nancy*, 256.
107 Ibid., 261.

by her tree patriarchs that they may easily be overlooked. Occasionally there is a magnificent personification of some of the smaller plants, as in this selection from "An October Ride" (1881):

I passed some stiff, straight mullein stalks which stood apart together in a hollow as if they wished to be alone. They always remind me of the rigid old Scotch Covenanters, who used to gather themselves together in companies, against the law, to worship God in some secret hollow of the bleak hill-side. Even the smallest and youngest of the mulleins was a Covenanter at heart; they all had put by their yellow flowers, and they will still stand there, gray and unbending, through the fall rains and winter snows, to keep their places as well-to-do, dignified citizens. It is not a question of soil and of location any more than it is with us....

It is impossible for one who has been a great deal among trees to resist the instinctive certainty that they have thought and purpose, and that they deliberately anticipate the future, or that they show traits of character which one is forced to call good or evil. How low down the scale of existence we may find the first glimmer of selfconsciousness nobody can tell. ...Man was the latest comer into this world, and he is just beginning to get acquainted with his neighbors, this is the truth of it.[108]

From this point Jewett observes that the primitive pagans were wrong in inventing an imaginary race of spirits to inhabit the trees. Trees have their own souls and personalities that are analogous to, but not identical with, those of human beings. For this reason, she points out, "the true nature and life of a tree can never be exactly personified".

Because of the absence of plots in most of her stories, Jewett's personifications cannot be shown to have a dramatic function, yet they stand on an equal basis with many human characters serving as points of interest. Only occasionally does she attempt to lend a personality to nature as a whole. Though she sometimes uses, in a conventional way, the "mechanistic" phraseology of modern natural science, she never resigns her complete faith in a conventional teleological and dualistic world, in which the forces of nature are roughly identified with the will of the Author of the Universe. She may say casually that "Nature repossesses herself surely of what we boldly claim", but she does not neglect to add, in the same paragraph: "But it is only God who can plan and order it all, – who is father to his children, and cares for the least of us." The impact of modern natural science upon her mind may have stimulated her curiosity in botanical and biological knowledge, but always she conceived of natural law as "the thoughts which He writes for us in the book of Nature".[109] Her taste for the mystic aspect of plant life was hardly comparable to that of Allen, but occasionally a note of this kind is struck, as in a forest in "The Gray Man", where

There is everywhere a token of remembrance, of silence and secrecy. Some stronger nature once ruled these neglected trees and this fallow ground. They will wait the return of their master as long as roots can creep through mold, and make way for them. The stories of strange lives have been whispered to the earth, their thoughts have burned themselves into the cold rocks.[110]

Freeman's interest in personification presents a strange pattern of development. In her early period she employed a bold style devoid of almost all figures of speech; there is not one serious attempt in her entire first volume to bring a background object to life or endow it with a human-like individuality. *A New England Nun and Other Stories* is scarcely different in this respect. In fact, not before "Evelina's Garden" in *Silence and Other Stories* (1898), after Freeman has joined the nature school, does personification appear to any appreciable extent. In this story the flowers in the famous enclosure, the

hollyhocks, blooming in rank and file, seemed to be marching upon them [the spectators] like platoons of soldiers...; and, indeed, the whole garden seemed changing with its mass of riotous bloom upon the hedge. They could scarcely take in details of marigold and phlox and pinks and London-pride and cock's-combs, and prince's feathers waving overhead like standards.[111]

Later in the story one meets "the mysterious gloom of the bushes", whence came "the twangs of the katydids, like some coarse quarrellers, each striving for the last word in a dispute not even dignified by excuse of passion".[112]

---

[109] *Deephaven*, 187.
[110] *A White Heron and Other Stories*, 25; see also *The King of Folly Island*, 211, and *The Best Stories of Sarah Orne Jewett*, Willa Cather, ed. (Boston, 1925), 213.
[111] *Silence*, 111-12.
[112] Ibid., 135.

In *Understudies* (1901) the principal characters, as previously stated, are mostly small animals, ingeniously endowed with human-like courage, loyalty, and perseverance. "The Cat", for example, has no lack of acute perception and intelligence, though "his reasoning was always sequential and circuitous". He did not speculate about the future: "always for him what had been would be, and the more easily for his marvellous waiting powers".[113] "The Lost Dog", who leaves a kind master for a former unappreciative one out of sheer loyalty, may have gained, the author tells us, "another level in the spiritual evolution of his race".[114] Here Freeman has begun to drop her objectivity and to theorize with mixed ethical, semi-mystical, and even scientific notions. *Six Trees* (1903) carries on in precisely the same vein, with a growing tendency toward personification. These tree personalities are reminiscent of Jewett:

It was in the summer-time that the great pine sang his loudest song of winter.... In the winter the tree seemed to sing of the slumberous peace under his gently fanning boughs, and the deep swell of his aromatic breath in burning noons.[115]

The tree stood alone. He stood quiescent with the wind in his green plumes. He belonged to that simplest form of life which cannot project itself beyond its own existence to judge of it.[116]

The tree... loomed over him like a prophet with solemnly waving arms of benediction, prophesying in a great unknown language of his own.[117]

There had been five in the family of the Lombardy poplar. Formerly he had stood before the Dunn house in a lusty row of three brothers and a mighty father, from whose strong roots, extending far under the soil, they had all grown.

Now they were all gone, except this one, the last of the sons of the tree. He alone remained, faithful as sentinel before the onslaught of winter storms and summer suns; he yielded to neither. He was head and shoulders above the other trees – the cherry and horse-chestnuts in the square front yard behind him. Higher than the house, piercing the blue with his broad truncate of green, he stood silent, stiff, and immovable.[118]

113 *Understudies*, 7.
114 Ibid., 61.
115 *Six Trees*, 69.
116 Ibid., 73.
117 Ibid., 78.
118 Ibid., 131-32.

The whole tree seemed to pant, and sing, and shout with perfume; it seemed to call even more loudly than the robins that lived in its boughs. The tree was utter perfection, and a triumph over all around it.[119]

In the later volumes, Freeman's personifications are limited to briefer figures, which might be said to characterize all her stories after she became an imitator of the nature writers. Her personifications are not so convincing as Jewett's, yet she occasionally involves them in dramatic situations in a story.

With Eggleston, the use of personified setting is so rare as to be almost foreign to his style. A few exceptional figures that give life to natural objects may be found, such as "The great backlog, hoary with gray ashes, lay slumbering at the back of the fireplace";[120] "the high hills... stood sentinels on every hand about the valley in which New Geneva stood";[121] and "the dark maples were threatening giants against the sky".[122] However much Eggleston may have been preoccupied with his own natural surroundings, he seems never to have made a literary use of nature other than as an aesthetic picture or an influence upon human thought and feeling.

In Garland's stories, as in those of Eggleston, personification of natural backgrounds is more exceptional than characteristic. Though Garland was to some extent a poet, and is sometimes credited with a quality of poetic imagination in his prose,[123] his association with nature remained aesthetic and exterior rather than intimate and mystical, and he did not often search out the souls of the lower forms of life about him, as did Allen and Jewett. His use of personified setting is therefore limited to a few short figures of speech, such as the following:

All nature seemed to declare a day of rest, and invited men to disassociate ideas of toil from the rustling green wheat, shining grass, and tossing blooms.[124]

---

[119] Ibid., 174.
[120] *Duffels*, 29.
[121] Ibid., 161.
[122] "Ben: A Story for May-Day", 75.
[123] Maurice Hewlett, "Biography and Memoirs", *The London Mercury*, VII, 106 (November, 1922).
[124] Ibid., 291.

The water came down over its dam with a leap of buoyant joy, as if leaping to freedom.[125]

It [the burnt mill] seemed like the charred body of a living thing, this heap of blackened and twisted shafts and pulleys lying half buried in tangles of weeds.[126]

Though simple personification, at the level of figurative language, is found in all literary art, the American local colorists, in their desire to coax all of the delicacies of emotion from their landscapes, moved farther and took greater artistic risks than most of their predecessors or followers. Harte and Murfree venture extensively into this field of experimentation, sometimes achieving a remarkable and delicious subtlety and sometimes failing by heavy handedness.

Some of the group were too fearful of pathetic fallacy to take the risks of personifications; Twain would have no part of scenic personification in his fiction, though he indulged himself often and deeply enough in his travel pieces. Page, Eggleston and Garland were simply not interested; they expended their experimental efforts in other directions. Freeman, especially in her later work, was more like and came closer to Jewett than her critics are aware. Those venturing farthest were Allen and Jewett; Allen obviously went too far and Jewett too frequently into the treacherous borderland between place and person. Of the two, Jewett was more successful in preserving the integrity of her art. The fact that her narrative art was more reflective than dramatic proved greatly to her advantage in the animation of her scenes.

[125] Hamlin Garland, *Wayside Courtships* (New York, 1897).
[126] Ibid., 204.

5

CONCLUSION

Through the preceding chapters references have been frequently made to the critical judgments of historians and critics interested in the American local color movement and a number of discrepancies have been noted. The evidence presented in the preceding chapters brings into question Carl Van Doren's statement that the local colorists were not "much differentiated among themselves by highly individual ideas or methods".[1] On this evidence, moreover, Wann's definition of local color in terms of an emphasis on typical scenery, typical costume, and typical dialect,[2] is hardly satisfactory, for the scenery used by the local colorists as a whole is not typical, but individual and particular. Granville Hicks'[3] objection to the backward tendency in local color, to its propensity to escape from reality rather than to attend to the new conditions of industrial urban life, is justified only by his own assumption that literary attainment is to be judged by an author's responsiveness to forces of economic determinism. His general disapprobation of the regional fiction of the period is a result of an evaluation based upon the whole unselected mass of experimental writing, rather than upon the few classics that represent its highest level. With further selectivity local color fiction need not suffer by comparison with the representative work of earlier periods of our literary history. A. H. Quinn's conception of the local color movement as the rediscovery by Americans of "the romance that lay around them" practically identifies the movement with the work of pre-war ro-

---

[1] Carl Van Doren, *The American Novel*, revised and enlarged, 203.
[2] Wann, op. cit., 10.
[3] Hicks, op. cit., 66-67.

manticists, and ignores somewhat the essential novelty of the new school.[4] G. Harrison Orians, historian and co-editor of an anthology of American local color stories, is the only critic noticed who recognizes the interest of local colorists in "environmental factors" and "other essential features as they affected character". He also rightly observes that the average local colorist "focused attention upon background or setting", and that "upon the accurate portrayal of this setting, whether of city or mountainside, much of his success depends".[5]

As has been stated in the opening chapter, all local colorists of the period have a single important feature in common, an absorbing interest in landscapes, scenery, or nature, whether *a priori* or imitative, and a tendency toward an inordinate preoccupation with setting as a part of their narrative technique. Among the representative authors discussed in this study, who were better than average local colorists, the treatment which setting received is more impressive for its variety than its triteness, and suggests, apart from the ample personal testimony, a remarkable experimentation with and development of the story of setting.

Also pointed out in the preliminary chapter was the difficulty of interpreting the local color movement as a mixture of romanticism and realism, or as a transitory stage between these two major movements; such an hypothesis is too simple an explanation for the facts presented in this study. There is a new element in local color fiction which could never have been derived from any combination of realism and romanticism, however loosely the terms are used. This new element may be described as a bias in literary method which makes the revelation of a particular time and place more important than either an escape from reality or a fidelity to universal law of abstract truth. A study of setting in the local color stories shows that the best writers in the local color school were not lazily and subserviently following a popular vogue; whether they expressed their theories or not, they were conscious experimenters, and no two authors had quite the same technique for reaching the common goal of setting down the essence of a locality

---

[4] Quinn, op. cit., 373.
[5] Orians, *A Short History of American Literature*, 216-17.

which they knew. With this aim in mind, it is only natural that they should make use of typical characters, and typical dress, speech, manners, and actions; but only rarely can the settings themselves be called typical. Though there is indeed some repetition in setting, it is generally found only within the work of a particular author. This is to be explained by the fact that successful experimentation could not come from careless manipulation of all elements in a story form at once; during the local color period, while experimentation lay in the direction of setting, the other elements of the story tended to remain constant. Such condition is a requisite of any experimental process.

Since local color fiction was experimental, it is only natural that numerous failures should occur for every successful innovation. Critics who are inclined to sneer at the artificiality of local color artists should bear in mind that their successful efforts have not yet been adequately separated from their unsuccessful ones. Pattee has gone far toward selecting the grain from the chaff, ending with a discovery of perhaps a dozen volumes of stories fit for the most exclusive shelf of American classics. It is only fair and just that the local colorists, like other authors, should be evaluated from the standpoint of their successful rather than their unsuccessful works.

Considering the nature of these experiments more closely, one can see several trends which fit into the intellectual picture of America during the period. (1) The popularity of detailed and colorful landscape paintings, largely stimulated by Jean Francois Millet (1814-1875) and a school of Dutch painters, fostered an aesthetic tradition in America which embraced the pictorial in all forms of art. (2) The new national consciousness after the war was marked by a semi-patriotic interest and intense curiosity in the isolated regions of the country. (3) The common goal of national literary independence was still a conscious drive, and promoted the rise of local, native artists who claimed to have lost contact with Eastern and European convention and tradition. (4) A new interest in travel literature,[6] which had never actually died out from Colonial days, was stimulated by the large migrations in

---

[6] The traveller-reporter tradition is especially evident in the descriptive sketches of Twain, Cable, and Allen.

America immediately before and after the war. (5) A new school of nature writers, led by Burroughs, Muir, and Miller, arose in the eighties and nineties to take the place of Emerson and Thoreau. (6) Darwinian and Spencerian thought, which was being interpreted to the American mind at this time through such works as John Fiske's *Outlines of Cosmic Philosophy Based on the Doctrine of Evolution* (1874), promoted a serious interest in environment and fostered a scientific point of view in all kinds of literary expression. (7) The rise of a natural and social science based on a deterministic and mechanistic point of view worked in opposition to the American frontier ideal of manifest destiny and other optimistic prophecies of a glorious future. Each of these tendencies is not only evident in the content of the American short story of the period, but is also recognized as a psychological factor which helped to fix the directions of experimentation.

Illustrations will hardly be necessary, except perhaps in the case of the element last mentioned – the rise of naturalism – which deserves further emphasis. Some aspect of the gradual impact of naturalism upon the descriptive use of scenic backgrounds may be seen in the work of almost all of the local colorists. In its earlier stages it is apparent in Twain and Allen; in its more mature stages in Freeman and Garland. Allen and Garland portrayed not merely the outward manifestations of their localities, but the deeper structures as well; and they made use of scientific and sociological theses not so much, as some critics believe, in the interest of transcendental or universal truth[7] as in an effort to give a definitive particularization of their respective localities.

Historians have not yet noticed to what extent the local colorists as a whole were preoccupied with philosophical ideas as the rationale of their literary innovations in the use of landscapes or nature in general. Though Pattee, Hicks, Quinn, Wann, Van Doren, and other critics have been very cognizant of the more political, moral, and sectionalistic theses among the local colorists, they have not noticed, generally, that these authors were scientific in their conceptions of the relation of man to his environment. One has

[7] Parrington, *The Beginnings of Critical Realism*, 292.

only to consider the rational hylozoism in Jewett's dissertation on tree folk[8] to see how philosophically alert were some of the exuberant and spontaneous landscape artists.

It would not be correct to refer to local colorists generally as naturalists any more than to call them romantics or realists, for they were all of these and more. They were interpreters of American localities, and their particular points of view and methods of interpretation were individualistic and varied, ranging all the way from ecstatic subjective description to the most objective scientific analysis and scholarly documentation. The local color movement was a self-conscious development, with its own leaders and critics, and its experimentation was as systematic as that of almost any other literary school that has arisen in America.

It is necessary to view the data of this study collectively within its three categories in order to gather its full significance. The general prevalence of the more important functions of setting in the stories of the various authors selected tends to dispel, first of all, the prevailing notion that the local colorists as a whole used setting chiefly as a mere background or ornament, as the decorative stage setting in a theater. Actually, this type of setting is found only in the poorer work of Harte, Murfree, and in the work of minor representatives not incorporated in this study.[9] Cable made an extensive use of independent setting, but he worked according to a highly developed technique whereby he sought to reinforce the mood or suspense of the narrative by adding to it the emotional effect of interpolated descriptions. Jewett made use of long and intrusive descriptions of scenery mainly to reveal deep and intimate impressions of all the stages of life about her. Jewett, like most other local colorists, was working away from the traditional notion of Matthews and others that the short story must be a structural unity based upon a highly dramatic situation; she was learning, like

[8] Jewett, *Country By-Ways*, 163-70.
[9] A secondary list of local colorists who worked extensively in the field of the short story would probably include Joel Chandler Harris, Kate Chopin, Grace King, and F. Hopkinson Smith for the South; Harriet Beecher Stowe, Elizabeth Stuart, Phelps Ward, Rose Terry Cooke, and Alice Brown for New England; and Rebecca Harding Davis, Alice French, Constance Fenimore Woolson, and Margaret Deland for the Middle West.

Cable, to make use of an emotional unity based upon atmospheric effects. The expert selectivity of descriptive details in the work of Page proved the possibility for a great efficiency in this type of technique, though Page was primarily an advocate of strong plots. Obviously not all attempts to use independent atmospheric setting as an aesthetic force upon the reader's imagination were successful, for there are failures enough among the best artists; but the stronger writers, especially Cable, have demonstrated that a story sometimes can be strengthened as well as weakened by long descriptions.

When one observes the data of the second category, setting in close relation to character, the most important thing to be noticed, as already discussed, is the seriousness with which these writers treated the idea of environment, the extent to which they reflected the new natural and social science, and the sincerity with which they distinguished their respective localities. Also noticeable is the influence of Hawthornesque parallelism upon the movement; Murfree, Allen, and Freeman have all carried the symbolical impulse into their use of setting and character. A third phenomenon should be mentioned: the use of a mystical relation between man and nature, found chiefly in Allen and Jewett. It was comparatively late in appearing, being largely an influence from the nature school of the nineties.

The third category, personified setting, reveals a remarkable individuality among the various authors. Harte, Murfree, and Allen all worked extensively in this hazardous realm, but so different were their methods that almost no generalization can be made, except perhaps that all three were so much interested in setting as sometimes to place it in a major role. Here may be seen one aspect of the local color movement that is definitely not stereotyped or imitative. Harte's treatment of Roaring Camp, Murfree's Witch-Face Mountain, and Allen's Mother Nature are all remarkable personifications. All three writers were experimenting toward the same general objective; yet the different techniques that they employed deny any imputation of conscious mutual influence.

The geographical or regional aspect of the problem favors the general thesis that the American local color movement was primarily a cooperative literary interpretation of scenes, landscapes, and general environment of distinctive localities, achievable either through simple description, through various literary techniques, through the common features of the humanity a region has produced. If the local colorists were merely superficial observers, how does it happen that the stories of each region generally have more in common in tone and point of view, if not structure, than stories of different regions? Influence, or imitation, is partly responsible, but there is apparently something about a region itself, about either its physical aspect or its past history, which determines somewhat the literary treatment it receives at the hand of an authoritative interpreter. The more successful local colorists, most of whom were natives, were sensitive to the emotional values of their surroundings as well as their spectacular values; superficiality in landscaping was more characteristic of amateurs and tourists than genuine artists. The homogeneity of the best stories pertaining to each of the major regions should be taken as a strong evidence of artistic fidelity on the part of the authors to both the conspicuous and the inconspicuous features of their regions, and should discourage the attitude that they searched for the quaint, picturesque, and unique instead of the normal and representative.

The chronological aspect of the movement further shows that its chief trend was toward a more adequate portrayal of locality. During the seventies Harte and Eggleston were already showing a distinct partiality for individualized setting rather than individualized character, but they were somewhat Hawthornesque and Dickensian in their use of this element. Their settings tended to be sentimental, artificial, general rather than particular, and sometimes inadequately related to the rest of the story. Within the next decade, however, setting was given not only more emphasis and space, but also more significant functions in the story. Cable was gaining considerable headway in this new device for atmospheric power, Murfree was assigning character roles to her woods and mountains, Allen was beginning to use scientific and mystical ideas as a rationale for his settings, and Freeman and Garland were developing new sociological points of view toward environment which gave setting a new and unprecedented importance in the story. The nineties saw the maturity of the experiments of the eighties, and a greater infusion into the short stories of ideas of naturalism, which had previously appeared chiefly in the novel. As the century approached its conclusion, the short story which specialized in setting came to vie in popularity with stories of plot and character. During the three decades after the war, setting as an element of narration rose from a place of obscurity to full equality with plot and character, largely as a result of the experimentation with this element by the numerous local colorists. A new type of short story, the story of setting, stands as their chief contribution to American letters.

BIBLIOGRAPHY

INDIVIDUAL AUTHORS

JAMES LANE ALLEN

Primary Sources

The Blue-Grass Region of Kentucky and Other Sketches (New York, The Macmillan Co., 1900).
The Bride of the Mistletoe (New York, The Macmillan Co., 1909).
"Certain Criticisms of Certain Tales", *The Century Magazine*, XLII, 153-54 (May, 1891).
The Doctor's Christmas Eve (New York, The Macmillan Co., 1910).
Flute and Violin and Other Kentucky Tales and Romances (New York, The Macmillan Co., 1908).
A Kentucky Cardinal and Aftermath (New York, The Macmillan Co., 1928).
"Local Color", *The Critic*, VIII, 13-14 (January 9, 1886).
Summer in Arcady (New York, The Macmillan Co., 1902).
"Too Much Momentum", *Harper's New Monthly Magazine*, LXX, 701-710 (April, 1885).

Secondary Sources

Anonymous, "The Choir Invisible", *Saturday Review*, LXXXIV, 19 (July 3, 1897).
——, A Review of "A Summer in Arcady", *Saturday Review*, LXXXIII, 204 (February 20, 1897).
Bottorff, William K., *James Lane Allen* (New York, Twayne Publishers, 1964).
Bradley, William A., "James Lane Allen's *The Doctor's Christmas Eve*", *The Bookman*, XXXII, 641 (February 11, 1911).
Hancock, A. E., "The Art of James Lane Allen", *The Outlook*, LXXIV, 953-55 (August 15, 1903).
Knight, Grant C., *James Lane Allen and the Genteel Tradition* (Chapel Hill, The University of North Carolina Press, 1935).
MacArthur, James, "A Note on Mr. James Lane Allen", *The Bookman*, V, 288-90 (June, 1897).
Nelson, J. H., "James Lane Allen", in *The Dictionary of American Biography*, I, 195-96.
Payne, D. W., Jr., "The Stories of James Lane Allen", *The Sewanee Review*, VIII, 45-55 (January, 1900).

Scudder, H. E., "Mr. Allen's *The Choir Invisible*", The Atlantic Monthly, LXXX, 144 (July, 1897).

Sherman, Ellen Burns, "The Works of James Lane Allen", *The Book Buyer*, XX, 374-77 (June, 1900).

Townsend, John Wilson, *Kentucky in American Letters, 1784-1912*, Two volumes (Cedar Rapids, Iowa, The Torch Press, 1913).

GEORGE WASHINGTON CABLE

Primary Sources

"Art and Morals in Books", *Independent*, XLXX, 1643-44 (December 16, 1899).

Bonaventure (New York, Charles Scribner's Sons, 1888).

The Cable Story Book (New York, Charles Scribner's Sons, 1911).

"A Charming Old Gentleman", *The Book Buyer*, XXI, 378-80 (December, 1900).

"Drop Shot", *The Daily Picayune*, July 3 and 17, 1870. Original in *Times-Picayune* Office. From a copy of a typescript gift of Mr. Edward Stone.

"Drop Shot", *The Weekly Picayune*, March 26, 1870. Original at Texas A. and M. College. From a copy of a photostat gift of Mr. James C. Watson.

Old Creole Days (New York, Charles Scribner's Sons, 1892).

"*Posson Jone'*" and Pere Raphael (New York, Charles Scribner's Sons, 1909).

"Speculations of a Story-Teller", *The Atlantic Monthly*, LXXVII, 88-96 (July, 1896).

Strong Hearts (New York, Charles Scribner's Sons, 1908).

Secondary Sources

Bickle, Lucy Leffingwell Cable, *George Washington Cable, His Life and Letters* (New York, Charles Scribner's Sons, 1928).

Butcher, Charles Phillip, *George W. Cable: The Northhampton Years* (New York, Columbia University Press, 1959).

Butcher, Charles P., *George Washington Cable* (New York, Twayne Publishers, 1962).

King, Grace, A Review of *Monsieur Motte*, The Nation, XLVII, 95 (August 2, 1888).

Rubin, Louis Decinnus, *George W. Cable: Life and Times of A Southern Heretic* (New York, Pegasus, 1969).

Turner, Arlin, *George W. Cable, A Biography* (Durham, Duke University Press, 1956).

SAMUEL LANGHORNE CLEMENS

Primary Sources

Mark Twain's Letters, Edited by A. B. Paine, Two volumes (New York, Harper and Brothers, 1917).

Roughing It, Two volumes (New York, Harper and Brothers, n.d.).
Mark Twain's Works, Mississippi Edition, Twenty-two volumes (New York and London, Harper and Brothers, 1923-24).

Secondary Sources

Anonymous, A Review of *Roughing It, The Overland Monthly*, VIII, 580-81 (June, 1872).
Clemens, Clara, *My Father Mark Twain* (New York and London, Harper and Brothers, 1931).
Degroot, Henry, A Series of Articles on the Mining Industry in the Far West, *The Overland Monthly*, IX, 401-12 (November, 1870); X, 489-500 (June, 1873).
Herron, Ima, *The Small Town in American Literature* (Durham, Duke University Press, 1939).
Johnson, Merle, *A Bibliography of Mark Twain* (New York, Harper and Brothers, 1935).
Paine, A. B., *Mark Twain: A Biography*, Three volumes (New York, Harper and Brothers, 1912).
Rogers, Franklin R., *Mark Twain's Burlesque Patterns* (Dallas, Southern Methodist University Press, 1960).
Smith, Henry N., *Mark Twain* (Englewood, New Jersey: Prentice-Hall, 1963).
——, *Mark Twain: Development of a Writer* (Cambridge, Harvard University Press, 1962).
Wagenknecht, Edward C., *Mark Twain, The Man and His Work* (Norman, Oklahoma, University Press, 1961).

EDWARD EGGLESTON

Primary Sources

"Ben: A Story for May-Day", Scribner's Monthly, II, 71-77 (May, 1871).
Duffels (New York, D. Appleton and Co., 1893).
The End of the World, A Love Story (New York, Orange Judd and Co., 1872).
"Formative Influences", *The Forum*, X, 279-90 (November, 1890).
The Hoosier Schoolmaster, A Story of the Backwoods Life in Indiana (New York, The Macmillan Co., 1928).
The Schoolmaster's Stories for Boys and Girls (Boston, Henry L. Shepherd and Co., 1874).

Secondary Sources

Anonymous, A Review of *The Hoosier Schoolmaster, The Nation*, XIV, 44-46 (January 18, 1872).
——, "The Author of 'Roxy'", *The Book Buyer*, IV, 96-97 (April, 1887).

Auringer, O. C., "Dr. Eggleston at Lake George", *The Critic*, XI, 111-112 (September 3, 1887).

Carey, Edward, "Dr. Edward Eggleston", *The Book Buyer*, XXV, 221-23 (October, 1902).

Eggleston, George Carey, *Recollections of a Varied Life* (New York, Henry Holt and Co., 1910).

Flanagan, John T., "The Hoosier Schoolmaster in Minnesota", Minnesota History, 347-70 (December, 1937).

Nicholson, Meredith, "Edward Eggleston", *The Atlantic Monthly*, XC, 804-809 (December, 1902).

Randel, William Pierce, *Edward Eggleston* (New York, King's Crown Press, 1946).

Riddle, Drexel, "The First of the Hoosiers", *The Outlook*, LXXVIII, 382-83 (October 8, 1904).

Rusk, Robert L., "Edward Eggleston", *The Dictionary of American Biography*, VI, 52-54.

Tooker, L. F., "Fiction of the Magazines", *The Century*, CVIII, 260-71 (June, 1924).

MARY ELEANOR WILKINS FREEMAN

Primary Sources

Edgewater People (New York, Harper and Brothers, 1918).

The Fair Lavinia and Others (New York, Harper and Brothers, 1907).

The Givers (New York, Harper and Brothers, 1904).

A Humble Romance and Other Stories (New York, Harper and Brothers, 1915).

The Love of Parson Lord and Other Stories (New York, Harper and Brothers, 1900).

"New England, 'Mother of America'", *Country Life in America*, XXII, 27-32; 64-70 (July 1, 1912).

A New England Nun and Other Stories (New York, Harper and Brothers, 1919).

People of Our Neighborhood (Philadelphia, Curtis Publishing Co., 1898).

Silence and Other Stories (New York, Harper and Brothers, 1898).

Six Trees (New York, Harper and Brothers, 1903).

Understudies (New York, Harper and Brothers, 1901).

The Wind in the Rosebush (New York, Doubleday, Page, and Co., 1903).

The Winning Lady (New York and London, Harper and Brothers, 1909).

Young Lucretia and Other Stories (New York, Harper and Brothers, 1892).

Secondary Sources

Anonymous, "A Writer of New England", The Nation, XCI, 386-87 (October 27, 1910).

——, "Mary E. Wilkins", *The Critic*, XX, 13 (January 2, 1892).

Chamberlain, Joseph Edgar, "Miss Mary E. Wilkins at Randolph, Massachusetts", *The Critic*, XXXII, 156-58 (March 5, 1898).

Dobson, Willis, "The Responsiveness of Mary E. Wilkins to Public Taste During the Years 1896-1901", Unpublished MS., 1939.

Macy, John, "The Passing of the Yankee", *The Bookman*, LXXXII, 616-21 (August, 1931).
Matthiessen, F. O., "New England Stories", in *American Writers on American Literature*, Edited by John Macy, (New York, Horace Liveright, Inc., 1921).
More, Paul Elmer, "Hawthorne: Looking Before and After", Independent, LVI, 1489-94 (June, 1904).
Moss, Mary, "Some Representative American Story Tellers", *The Bookman*, XXIV, 21-29 (September, 1906).
Pratt, Cornelia Atwood, "Notes of a Novel-Reader", *The Critic*, XXXVII, 274-76 (September, 1900).
Thompson, C. M., "Miss Wilkins, an Idealist in Masquerade", *The Atlantic Monthly*, LXXXII, 665-75 (May, 1899).
Westbrook, Perry D., *Mary Wilkins Freeman* (New York, Twayne Publishers, 1967).
Williams, Blanche Colton, *Our Short Story Writers* (New York, Moffat, Yard, and Co., 1920).

HAMLIN GARLAND

Primary Sources

Crumbling Idols (Chicago and Cambridge, Stone and Kimball, 1894).
A Daughter of the Middle Border (New York, The Macmillan Co., 1921).
"Limitations of Authorship in America", *The Bookman*, LIX, 257-62 (May, 1924).
A Little Norsk, or Old Pap's Flaren (New York, D. Appleton and Co., 1892).
Main-Travelled Roads, New Edition (New York and London, Harper and Brothers, 1899).
"Meetings with Howells", *The Bookman*, XLX, 1-7 (March, 1917).
"The Middle West – Heart of the Country", *Country Life in America*, XXII, 19-24; 44-46 (September 15, 1912).
"My Friend John Burroughs", *The Century Magazine*, CII, 731-42 (September, 1921).
My Friendly Contemporaries; A Literary Log (New York, The Macmillan Co., 1932).
Other Main-Travelled Roads (New York and London, Harper and Brothers, 1910).
"Pioneers and City Dwellers", *The Bookman*, LVIII, 369-72 (December, 1923).
Prairie Folks (New York and London, Harper and Brothers, 1899).
Prairie Songs (Cambridge and Chicago, Stone and Kimball, 1893).
"Sanity in Fiction", *The North American Review*, CLXXVI, 336-48 (March, 1903).
They of the High Trails (New York and London, Harper and Brothers, 1916).
Wayside Courtships (New York, D. Appleton and Co., 1897).

Secondary Sources

Anonymous, "New Figures in Literature and Art: Hamlin Garland", *The Atlantic Monthly*, LXXVI, 840-44 (December, 1895).
Bowen, Edwin W., "Hamlin Garland, the Middle-West Short Story Writer", *The Sewanee Review*, XXVII, 411-22 (October, 1919).

Hazard, Lucy Lockwood, *The Frontier in American Fiction* (New York, Thomas Y. Crowell Co., 1927).

Hewlett, Maurice, "Biography and Memoirs", *The London Mercury*, VII, 106 (November, 1922).

Holloway, Jean, *Hamlin Garland, A Biography* (Austin, University of Texas Press, 1960).

Howells, William Dean, "Mr. Garland's Books", *North American Review*, CXCVI, 523-28 (October, 1912).

O'Connor, Richard, *Bret Harte: A Biography* (Boston, Little Brown, 1966).

Pizer, Donald, *Hamlin Garland's Early Work and Career* (Berkeley, University of California Press, 1960).

Raw, Ruth M., "Hamlin Garland, the Romanticist", *The Sewanee Review*, XXXVI, 202-10 (April, 1928).

Van Doren, Carl, "The Roving Critic", *The Nation*, CXIV, 622 (May, 1922).

Williams, Blanche Carlton, *Our Short Story Writers* (New York, Moffat, Yard, and Co., 1920).

FRANCIS BRET HARTE

Primary Sources

Novels and Stories, Ten volumes, Fireside Edition (Boston and New York, no publisher, 1910).

Sketches of the Sixties (Mark Twain, co-author), Edited by John Howell, from *The Californian*, 1846-47 (San Francisco, J. Howell, 1927).

The Writings of Bret Harte, Twenty volumes, Riverside Edition (Boston and New York, Houghton Mifflin Co., 1910).

Secondary Sources

Anonymous, A Review of *Mrs. Skagg's Husbands and Other Sketches*, *The Overland Monthly*, X, 390-92 (April, 1873).

Boynton, Percy H., *The Rediscovery of the Frontier* (Chicago, University of Chicago Press, 1931).

May, E. R., "Bret Harte and the Overland Monthly", *American Literature*, XXII (November, 1950).

Merwin, Henry Childs, *The Life of Bret Harte, with Some Account of the California Pioneers* (Boston and New York, Houghton Mifflin Co., 1911).

SARAH ORNE JEWETT

Primary Sources

Country By-Ways (Boston, Houghton and Co., 1881).

The Country of the Pointed Firs, in *The Best Stories of Sarah Orne Jewett*, Two volumes (Boston and New York, Houghton Mifflin Co., 1925).

Deephaven (Boston and New York, Houghton Mifflin Co., 1919).

The King of Folly Island and Other People (Boston and New York, Houghton Mifflin Co., 1888).

Letters of Sarah Orne Jewett, Edited by Annie Fields (Boston and New York, Houghton Mifflin Co., 1911).

The Life of Nancy (Boston and New York, Houghton Mifflin Co., 1896).

The Mate of the Daylight and Friends Ashore (Boston and New York, Houghton Mifflin Co., 1883).

A Native of Winby and Other Tales (Boston and New York, Houghton Mifflin and Co., 1893).

Old Friends and New (Boston and New York, Houghton Mifflin and Co., 1914).

The Queen's Twin and Other Stories (Boston and New York, Houghton Mifflin and Co., 1899).

Strangers and Wayfarers (Boston and New York, Houghton Mifflin and Co., 1896).

A White Heron and Other Stories (Boston and New York, Houghton Mifflin and Co., 1914).

Secondary Sources

Bishop, Ferman, *The Sense of the Past in Sarah Orne Jewett* (Wichita, Kansas, University of Wichita Press, 1959).

Cary, Richard, *Sarah Orne Jewett* (New York, Twayne Publishers, 1962).

Chapman, Edward M., "The New England of Sarah Orne Jewett", *Yale Review*, n.s., III, 157-72 (October, 1913).

Garnett, Edward, "Miss Sarah Orne Jewett's Tales", *The Academy*, LXV, 40 July 11, 1903).

Grattan, C. Hartley, "Sarah Orne Jewett", *The Bookman*, LXIX, 296-98 (May, 1929).

Matthiessen, Francis Otto, *Sarah Orne Jewett* (Boston and New York, Houghton Mifflin and Co., 1929).

——, "New England Stories", in *American Writers on American Literature*, Edited by John Macy (New York, Horace Liveright, Inc., 1921).

Rhode, Robert D., "Sarah Orne Jewett and 'The Palpable Present Intimate'", *Colby Library Quarterly*, VIII (September, 1968), 146-55.

Shackford, Martha, "Sarah Orne Jewett", *The Sewanee Review*, XXX, 20-26 (January, 1922).

Thompson, Charles Miner, "The Art of Miss Jewett", *The Atlantic Monthly*, XCIV, 485-97 (September, 1904).

Thorp, Margaret, *Sarah Orne Jewett* (Minneapolis, University of Minnesota Press, 1966).

MARY NOAILLES MURFREE

Primary Sources

The Bushwhackers and Other Stories (Chicago and New York, Herbert E. Stone and Co., 1899).
The Frontiersmen (Boston and New York, Houghton Mifflin and Co., 1904).
In the Tennessee Mountains (Boston and New York, Houghton Mifflin and Co., 1887).
The Mystery of Witch-Face Mountain (Boston and New York, Houghton Mifflin and Co., 1896).
The Phantoms of the Foot-Bridge and Other Stories (New York, Harper and Brothers, 1895).
The Young Mountaineers (Boston and New York, Houghton Mifflin and Co., 1897).

Secondary Sources

Anonymous, "Recent American Fiction", *The Atlantic Monthly*, LV, 121-32 (January, 1885).
——, "An American Story-Writer", *The Atlantic Monthly*, LIV, 131-33 (July, 1884).
Cary, Richard, *Mary N. Murfree* (New York, Twain Publishing Co., 1967).
Mooney, Mary Sue, *An Intimate Study of Mary Noailles Murfree* (Unpublished M. A. Thesis, George Peabody College for Teachers, 1929).
Parks, Edd Winfield, *Charles Egbert Craddock* (Chapel Hill, University of North Carolina Press, 1941).

THOMAS NELSON PAGE

Primary Sources

Bred in the Bone (New York, Charles Scribner's Sons, 1904).
The Burial of the Guns (New York, Charles Scribner's Sons, 1900).
Elskett, and Other Stories (New York, Charles Scribner's Sons, 1894).
In Old Virginia (New York, Charles Scribner's Sons, 1922).
"The South", *Country Life in America*, XXI, 43-48; 74-80 (April 1, 1912).
Under the Crust (New York, Charles Scribner's Sons, 1907).

Secondary Sources

Coleman, C. W., Jr., "The Recent Movement in Southern Literature", *Harper's Monthly*, LXXIV, 837-55 (May, 1887).
Earle, Mary Tracy, "A Romantic Chronicle", *The Book Buyer*, XVII, 297 (November, 1898).

Gordon, A. C., "Thomas Nelson Page", Scribner's Magazine, LXXIII, 75-80 (January, 1923).

Gross, Theodore L., *Thomas Nelson Page* (New York, Twayne Publishers, 1967).

Mims, Edwin, "Thomas Nelson Page", *The Atlantic Monthly*, C, 109-15 (July, 1907).

Nelson, J. H., "Thomas Nelson Page", *The Dictionary of American Biography*, XIV, 141-42.

Page, Rosewell, *Thomas Nelson Page* (New York, Charles Scribner's Sons, 1923).

GENERAL WORKS CITED

Anonymous, "Local Color and After", *The Nation*, CIX, 426-27 (September 27, 1919).

——, "Scenery in Fiction", *Littel's Living Age*, CCXXXV, 812-15 (December 27, 1902).

——, "Worship of Local Color", *The Nation*, LXXXIV, 75-76 (January 24, 1907).

Austin, Mary, "Regionalism in American Fiction", *The English Journal*, XXI, 97-107 (February, 1932).

Baring-Gould, S., "Color in Composition", *On the Art of Writing Fiction* (London, Wells, Gardner Dorton and Co., 1894).

Botkin, B. A., "Regionalism: Cult or Culture?" *English Journal*, XXV, 181-85 (March, 1936).

Brooke, Stopford, A., *Tennyson, His Art and Relation to Modern Life* (New York, G. P. Putnam's Sons, 1904).

The Cambridge History of American Literature, Edited by W. P. Trent, John Erskine, Stuart P. Sherman, and Carl Van Doren, Four volumes (New York, G. P. Putnam's Sons, 1917-21).

Cowie, Alexander, *The Rise of the American Novel* (New York, 1948).

Davidson, Donald, "Regionalism and Nationalism in American Literature", *The American Review*, V, 48-61 (April, 1935).

The Dictionary of American Biography, Edited by Allen Johnson and Dumas Malone (New York, Charles Scribner's Sons, 1928-37).

Dowden, Edward, *A History of French Literature* (London, William Heinemann, 1904).

Dyke, D. A., "Notes on Local Color and Its Relation to Realism", *College English*, XIV (November, 1952), 81-88.

Ellis, Havelock, "Love of Wild Nature", *The Contemporary Review*, XCV, 180-99 (February, 1909).

Ferril, T. H., "Writing in the Rockies; Religious Impulse, or Mysticism, Excited by Landscape", *The Saturday Review of Literature*, XV, 3-4; 13-14 (March, 1937).

Fiske, John, *Outlines of Cosmic Philosophy Based on the Doctrine of Evolution*, Two volumes, 13th edition (Boston and New York, Houghton Mifflin and Co., 1892).

Foerster, Norman, "Clerks of the Woods", *The Nation*, XCVII, 118-20 (August 7, 1913).

Herrick, Robert, "The Background of the American Novel", *The Yale Review*, III, 213-33 (January, 1914).

Hicks, Granville, *The Great Tradition, An Interpretation of American Literature Since the Civil War* (New York, The Macmillan Co., 1935).

House, Clyde Homer, *A Theory of the Genetic Basis of Appeal in Literature* (Lincoln, Nebraska, State Printing Co., n.d.).

Howells, William Dean, *Criticism and Fiction* (New York, no publisher, 1892).

James, W. P., "On the Theory and Practice of Local Color", *Littel's Living Age*, CCXIII, 743-48 (June 12, 1897).

Lathrop, Henry Burrowes, *The Art of the Novelist* (New York, Dodd, Mead and Co., 1919).

Lawton, William Cranston, "Local Color and Eternal Truth", *The Dial*, XXV, 38-39 (July 16, 1898).

Lieberman, Elias, *The American Short Story: A Study of the Influence of Locality in its Development* (Ridgewood, New Jersey, The Editor Co., 1912).

MacDowell, Tremaine, "Regionalism in American Literature", Minnesota History, XX, 105-18 (June, 1939).

Matthews, Brander, *The Philosophy of the Short Story* (New York, Longmans, Green and Co., 1917).

Orians, G. Harrison, *A Short History of American Literature Analyzed by Decades* (New York, F. S. Crofts and Co., 1940).

Parrington, Vernon Louis, *The Beginnings of Critical Realism in America*, 1860-1920 (New York, Harcourt Brace and Co., 1930) [Third volume of *Main Currents in American Thought*].

——, *The Romantic Revolution in America* (New York, Harcourt, Brace and Co., 1927) [Second volume of *Main Currents in American Thought*].

Pattee, Fred Lewis, *The Development of the American Short Story, An Historical Survey* (New York and London, Harper and Brothers, 1923).

——, *A History of American Literature Since 1870* (New York, The Century Co., 1916).

——, *Side Lights on American Fiction* (New York, The Century Co., 1922).

Perry, Bliss, "The Short Story", *The Atlantic Monthly*, XC, 241-52 (August, 1902).

——, *A Study of Prose Fiction* (New York, Houghton Mifflin Co., 1920).

Phillips, H. A., *Art in Short Story Narration* (New York, Stanhope-Dodge Publishing Co., 1913).

Pitkin, Walter B., *The Art and Business of Story Writing* (New York, The Macmillan Co., 1912).

Quinn, Arthur Hobson, *American Fiction. An Historical and Critical Survey* (New York, D. Appleton Century Co., 1936).

Rhode, Robert D., "Scenery and Setting: A Note on American Local Color", College English, XIII (Nov., 1951), 142-46.

Shaler, N. S., "Nature and Man in America", *Scribner's Magazine*, VIII, 361-76 (September, 1890).

Simpson, Claude M., ed., *The Local Colorists: American Short Stories, 1857-1900* (New York, Harper and Bros., 1960).

Symonds, John Addington, *Essays Speculative and Suggestive* (London, Smith, Elder and Co., 1907).

Tate, Allen, "Regionalism and Sectionalism", *The New Republic*, LXIX, 158-61 (December 23, 1931).

Taylor, Walter Fuller, *A History of American Letters* (Boston, American Book Co., 1936).

Van Doren, Carl, *The American Novel* (New York, The Macmillan Co., 1921).

——, *The American Novel*. Revised and enlarged (New York, The Macmillan Co., 1940).

——, *Contemporary American Novelists, 1900-1920* (New York, The Macmillan Co., 1922).

Wann, Louis, *The Rise of Realism: American Literature from 1860-1888* (New York, The Macmillan Co., 1937).

Webster's New International Dictionary (New York, G. and C. Merriam Co., 1934).

Weaver, R. M., "Realism and the Local Color Interlude", *Georgia Review*, XXII (Fall, 1968), 301-305.

Wedmore, Frederick, "The Short Story", *Littel's Living Age*, CCXVII, 392-400 (May 7, 1898).

INDEX

"Aftermath", 154, 156
The Alabaster Box, 63
Aldrich, Thomas Bailey, 35
"An Ali Baba of the Sierras", 142
"An Alien in the Pines", 133
Allen, James Lane, 10, 14, 17, 27, 34, 62-63, 73, 106-12, 135, 153-57, 158, 162, 164, 165, 168n, 169, 171
"Along Shore", 117
The American Claimant, 42
"An American Story Writer", 146n
"Among the Corn Rows", 128
"The Ancestors of Peter Atherly", 83
"A-Playing' of Old Sledge at the Settlemint", 148, 152
"Ash Can", 63
Atmosphere, 27, 30, 171
Audubon, John James, 155
"Au Large" (*Bonaventure*), 93, 95, 96
Austin, Mary, 30
Balzac, Honoré de, 13
"The Bar Light-House", 120
Baring-Gould, S., 15
"A Basement Story", 76
"Before the Low Green Door", 130
"Ben: A Story for May-day", 74, 126, 127n, 164n
"Bibi", 95
"A Bit of a Shore Life", 66, 159
Bonaventure, 95, 144n, 145n
"The Boom in the 'Calaveras Clarion'", 41
Botkin, B. A., 28

Boynton, Percy H., 87
"Brakes and White Vi 'lets", 119
"A Branch Road", 128
"The Brandon House", 64
Bred in the Bone, 106
"The Bride of the Mistletoe", 112
"A Brother to Diogenes", 105
Brown, Alice, 170n
"Brown of Calaveras", 40
The Burial of the Guns, 60, 103n, 104
Burlesque, 44
Burroughs, John, 77, 169
"The Bushwhacker", 55
"The Butterfly", 122
"By the Morning Boat", 116
Cable, George Washington, 10, 29, 34, 45, 46-54, 66, 73, 81, 92-98, 133, 135, 144-46, 168n, 170, 171, 172
The Cable Story Book, 95
"The Café des Exiles", 48, 145n
"The Californian's Tale", 91, 92
"Calla-Lilies and Hannah", 119, 120
"Captain Jim's Friend", 142
"Caranco", 92, 95
Carey, Richard, 99, 114n
"The Casting Vote", 100, 101
"The Cat", 73, 163
Cather, Willa, 117
"The Celebrated Jumping Frog of Calaveras County", 90, 92
Chateaubriand, François René, 13
Chopin, Kate, 170n

"The Christmas Peace", 60, 152
"Cinnamon Roses", 119
"A Convert of the Mission", 86
Cooke, Rose Terry, 170n
Country By-Ways, 65, 113, 158n, 159n, 161n, 162, 170
The Country of the Pointed Firs, 67, 117
Cowie, Alexander, 17
Craddock, Charles Egbert (See Mary Noailles Murfree), 146
"The Creamery Man", 129
"Cunner Fishing", 158
"A Cure for the Blues", 45
"The Dancin' Party at Harrison's Cove", 55, 98
Darwin, Charles, 27, 82, 169
Davidson, Donald, 28
Davis, Richard Harding, 170n
"A Day of Grace", 129
"A Day's Pleasure", 129
Deephaven, 64, 67, 117, 158, 162n
Defoe, Daniel, 18
Deland, Margaret, 170n
de Maupassant, Henri René Albert Guy, 19
Dickens, Charles, 19, 89, 172
Dike, D. A., 14
"A Discovered Pearl", 121
"A Doubled-Barreled Detective Story", 43, 75
Dreiser, Theodore, 127
"Drifting Crane", 128n, 130
"Drifting Down Lost Creek", 146, 152
Duffels, 74, 124n, 164n
Dutch painters, 168
Edgewater People, 123
Eggleston, Edward, 10, 36, 73-76, 124-27, 135, 164, 165, 172
"Elder Pill, Preacher", 129
"Electioneering on Big Injun Mounting", 99
Eliot, George, 19
Ellis, Havelock, 26
"Elsket", 103, 105, 152, 153n
Elsket, and Other Stories, 103n
"The Enemy Conquered", 45, 143
"An Esmeralda of Rocky Canon", 83
"The Esquimau Maiden's Romance", 43
"Evelina's Garden", 123, 162
"Fair Day", 116
"The Fair Lavinia", 124
The Fair Lavinia and Others, 73
Far West, 10, 31-33
"Farmer Finch", 65, 160
Ferril, T. H., 25, 26
Fielding, Henry, 18
Fields, Annie, 158
"Flip, A California Romance", 84, 88
"Flute And Violin", 62
Flute and Violin, 107, 108, 109, 110, 154n
Foerster, Norman, 25
Freeman, Mary E. (Wilkins), 10, 29, 35, 68-73, 118-24, 127, 131, 135, 162-64, 169, 171, 172.
French, Alice, 170n
Froebel, Friedrich, 125
Gabriel Conroy, 42
Garland, Hamlin, 10, 14, 15, 16, 17, 36, 76-81, 127-35, 164-65, 169
"A Gatherer of Simples", 118
Gautier, Theophile, 13
"George Washington's Last Duel", 59
Georgism, 130
The Givers, 123n, 124
"God's Ravens", 129
"Going to Shrewsbury", 116
"Grande Pointe", 95, 96
The Grandissimes, 95
"The Great Pine", 118
"The Gunpowder Plot", 124
Hardy, Thomas, 19, 140
"The 'Harnt' that Walks Chilhowee", 150, 152
Harris, Joel Chandler, 170n
Harte, Bret, 10, 31, 38-42, 82-90, 96, 135, 136, 138, 165, 170, 171, 172
Hawthorne, Nathaniel, 21, 31, 119, 171, 172
Hazard, Lucy, 129n
"Her Great-Grandmother's Ghost", 104
"The Heritage of Dedlow Marsh", 85

Herrick, Robert, 29
Hewlett, Maurice, "Biography and Memoirs", 164n
Hicks, Granville, 11, 166, 169
"High-Water Mark", 140, 141
"An Honest Soul", 120
House, Homer Clyde, 24, 26
"How I Went to the Mines", 83
"How Old Man Plunkett Went Home", 40
Howells, William Dean, 35, 130n
Hugo, Victor, 13
"Human interest", 24
"A Humble Romance", 68, 118n, 119n, 121n
A Humble Romance And Other Stories, 68
Hylozoism, 170
"The Idyll of Red Gulch", 38
In Ole Virginia, 105n
"In Shadow", 66, 158
In the Tennessee Mountains, 98, 99, 101, 102, 146, 149n
"In the Tules", 83
Irving, Washington, 21, 31
"A Jack and Jill of the Sierras", 83
"Jean-Ah Poquelin", 94, 133
Jewett, Sarah Orne, 10, 35, 64-67, 73, 81, 112-118, 135, 157-62, 163, 164, 165, 170, 171
"Jim's Big Brother from California", 87
"Joy", 124
"A Kentucky Cardinal", 154, 156
A Kentucky Cardinal and Aftermath, 155
King, Edward, 95
King, Grace, 170n
"The King of Folly Island", 116,
"King Solomon of Kentucky", 63
Knight, Grant C., 108, 109
Koslay, C. M., 39
"Lady Ferry", 64, 66, 113
"A Landless Farmer", 115
"Landocracy", 33
Landscape, 24
Lathrop, H. B., 18, 31
"Left Out on Lone Star Mountain", 41

Letters of Sarah Orne Jewett, 117n, 158
The Life of Nancy, 115, 160 n
"Little Darby", 57, 61
"The Little Maid at the Door", 72
Local color, 10, 12, 13-18, 81; Local color movement, 1, 5, 167, 172
Local Tradition, 27, 29
"The Long Hillside", 60
"The Lost Dog", 163
"A Lost Lover", 66
The Love of Parson Lord and Other Stories, 72
"The Luck of Roaring Camp", 39, 136, 138, 139
The Luck of Roaring Camp, and Other Sketches, 138
"Love Triumphant", 45
"Lucretia Burns", 128n, 129, 130, 133
MacDowell, Tremaine, 14
Macy, John, 72
"Madame Delicieuse", 48, 50, 146n
"Madame Delphine", 93, 144n, 145n
"A Maecenas of the Pacific Slope", 88, 142
Main-Travelled Roads, 78, 128, 131
"Mam' Lyddy's Recognition", 60
"Marse Chan", 58, 60
"Marsh Rosemary", 65
The Mate of the Daylight and Friend Ashore, 114n
Matthews, Brander, 21, 23, 170
Matthiessen, F. O., 34, 35n, 118
May, E. R., 138
"Meh Lady: A Story of the War", 59, 60
Middle West, 11, 36-37
"The Middle West-Heart of the Country", 77n
"Miggles", 86
Miller, Joaquin, 169
Millet, Jean François, 168
"A Millionaire of Rough and Ready", 85
Mims, Edwin, 57
"Miss Debby's Neighbors", 114
"Miss Godwin's Inheritance", 105, 153

"Miss Locke", 63

"M'liss", 87, 136

"The Moonshiners at Hobo-Hebee Falls", 151, 152

"Mountain-Laurel", 123

"Mrs. Ripley's Trip", 129

"Mrs. Skaggs' Husbands", 41

Muir, John, 169

Murfree, Mary Noailles (Charles Egbert Craddock), 10, 34, 45, 54-56, 73, 98-103, 133, 135, 146-52, 157, 165, 170, 171, 172

"My Cousin Fanny", 59

"My Metamorphosis", 38, 87

"The Mystery of Witch-Face Mountain", 148, 152

The Mystery of Witch-Face Mountain", 101

Natural scenery, 24-27

Nature, 24, 141, 153, 154, 155, 156, 157, 161, 162, 171

Naturalists, 82, 131, 170

"A Neighbor's Landmark", 115, 160

"The New Cashier", 126

New England, 10, 34-35

"New England, Mother of America", 118n

"A New England Nun", 121

A New England Nun and Other Stories, 70, 120n, 162

"A Night on the Divide", 83, 142

"No Haid Pawn", 104, 133

Norris, Frank, 127

Nostalgia, 34

"An October Ride", 113, 161

Old Creole Days, 94

Old Friends and New, 64, 113, 159n

"Old Jabe's Marital Experiments", 60

"Old Lady Pingree", 121

"Old 'Stracted' ", 104

Orians, G. Harrison, 167

Other Main-Travelled Roads, 78, 128, 129, 134

"The Outcasts of Poker Flat", 38, 86, 138, 139

"Over on T'Other Mounting", 133, 147, 152

"The Owner of the Mill Farm", 130

Page, Thomas Nelson, 10, 29, 34, 56-62, 81, 103-106, 133, 135, 152-53, 165, 171

Parrington, V. L., 11, 160n

"A Passage in the Life of Mr. John Oakhurst", 41

Pattee, Fred Lewis, 5, 11, 72n, 87, 88, 119n, 136, 167, 169

"Père Raphael", 52, 53

"Periwinkle", 126

Perry, Bliss, 18

Personification, 165, 171

Pestalozzi, Johann Heinrich, 125

"The Phantoms of the Foot Bridge", 99, 100, 151n

Phillips, H. A., 31

"Pinoneers and City Dwellers", 77n

Pitkin, Walter B., 27

Poe, Edgar Allan, 21

"A Poetess", 121

"Polly", 59

"Posson Jone", 49, 144n

"Posthumous Fame", 63

Prairie Folks, 79n, 128n, 130

"Priscilla", 74, 126

"The Queen's Twin", 114

Quinn, A. H., 10, 11, 166, 169

Raw, Ruth M., 77,

Realism, 14, 167, 170

"The Redemptioneer, A Story in Three Scenes", 75

Regionalism, 27, 28, 31-37

"The Reincarnation of Smith", 87

"The Return of a Private", 128

"The Revolt of Mother", 121

Rhode, Robert D., 6, 18, 157n

"River Driftwood", 113

"A Romance of the Line", 83

"The Romance of Sunrise Rock", 99, 100

Romanticism, 14, 167, 170

Roughing It, 91

Rousseau, Jean Jacques, 13, 20, 125

"Run to Seed", 103

"Salomy Jane's Kiss", 41

"A Sappho of Green Springs", 88

"Sarah Orne Jewett and 'The Palpable Present Intimate'", 157n

"The Scent of the Roses", 119, 120

The Schoolmaster's Stories, 76n

Sectionalism, 28

setting, 12, 18-27; As background and Ornament, 12, 20, 38-81; In Close Relation to Character, 12, 20, 82-135; Personified, 12, 20, 136-65

Shackford, Martha Hale, 67n

Short story, 12, 20-24

"Sieur George", 46, 145n

"Silence", 123, 162n

Silence and Other Stories, 72, 123, 162

Simpson, Claude M., 12

"Sister Dolorosa", 109, 111, 123, 154

"Sister Tabea", 74, 76

Six Trees, 118n, 124, 163

Smith, F. Hopkinson, 170n

"Snow Bound at the Eagle's", 87

"A Soldier of the Empire", 103

"The Solitary", 97, 144

A Son of the Middle Border, 77

South, 10, 32-34

"The Spectre in the Cart", 104

"Speculations of a Story-Teller", 145n

Spencer, Herbert, 125, 169

Spirit of the scene, 31

"The Squirrel", 122

"The Star of the Valley", 98, 102

"The Story of Bras-Coupe", 95

Stowe, Harriet Beecher, 35, 170n

Strangers and Wayfarers, 67n, 116n

Strong Hearts, 144n

Stuart, Elizabeth, 170n

"Summer in Arcady", 107, 111, 153, 156, 157

Summer in Arcady, 154n

Symbolism, 134, 158, 171

Symonds, John Addington, 25

"Taking the Blue Ribbon at the County Fair", 55

Tate, Allen, 28, 30

"Tennessee's Partner", 140

"Thankful Blossom," 143

Thoreau, Henry David, 155, 158

"Through the Santa Clara Wheat", 82

"Tite Poulette", 47

"Too Much Momentum", 62

Tradition, 28, 30

"The Tree of Knowledge", 72

Twain, Mark (Samuel L. Clemens), 5, 31, 37, 42-46, 75, 90-92, 135, 143-44, 165, 168n, 169

"The Twins of Table Mountain", 141

"Two Gentlemen of Kentucky", 107, 110

"Two Old Lovers", 68

"Uncle Tom at Home", 107

"Unc' Edinburg's Drowndin'", 58

Under the Crust, 160n, 153n

"Under the Lion's Paw", 128

Understudies, 73, 122, 123, 124, 163

"An Unwilling Guest", 119

"Up the Coolly", 128, 131, 133

Van Doren, Carl, 10, 36, 127, 128n, 166, 169

Wann, Louis, 1, 12, 166, 169

Ward, Phelps, 170n

Warfel, Harry R., 12

"Way Down in Lonesome Cove", 100

Wayside Courtships, 130, 165

Weaver, R. M., 14, 17

Wemore, Frederick, 21, 22

"What Is Man?", 90

"When the Waters Were Up at Jules", 82

"The White Cowl", 108, 109, 154

A White Heron and Other Stories, 65, 113, 115, 160

"The White Rose Road", 66

Whitman, Walt, 15

"William Bacon's Man", 129

"A Winter Drive", 65, 159

Woolson, Constance Fenimore, 170n

"The Work on Red Mountain", 38, 39, 87, 96

"The Youngest Miss Piper", 142

Zola, Emile, 13, 19, 21

Date Due

813.09   R47s

**HUNT LIBRARY
CARNEGIE-MELLON UNIVERSITY
PITTSBURGH, PENNSYLVANIA**

DEMCO